PERIODIC TABLE

INNOVATIONS

CHEMISTRY

for Curious Kids

An illustrated introduction to atoms, elements, chemical reactions, and more!

CRYSTALS

REACTIONS

IN THE LAB

MATERIALS

ARCTURUS

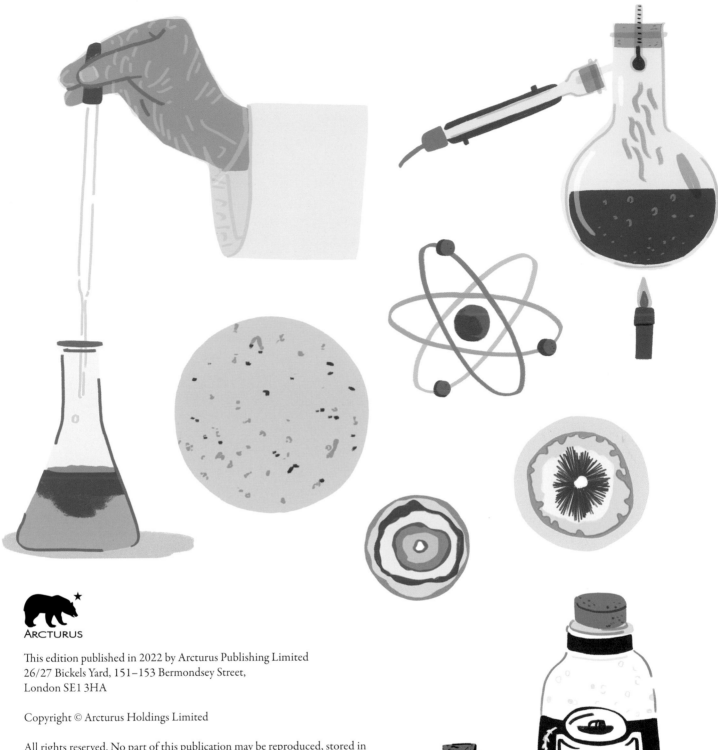

This edition published in 2022 by Arcturus Publishing Limited
26/27 Bickels Yard, 151–153 Bermondsey Street,
London SE1 3HA

Author: Lynn Huggins-Cooper
Illustrator: Alex Foster
Consultant: Anne Rooney
Designer: Jeanette Ryall
Packaged by Cloud King Creative

ISBN: 978-1-3988-0267-4
CH008270US
Supplier 29, Date 0822, PI 00001824

Printed in China

What is STEM?

STEM is a world-wide initiative that aims to cultivate an interest in
Science, Technology, Engineering, and Mathematics, in an effort to
promote these disciplines to as wide a variety of students as possible.

CONTENTS

THE AMAZING WORLD OF CHEMISTRY

Chemistry is the study of the "stuff" that the world is made from—**matter**. All matter is made from tiny building blocks called **atoms**. Chemistry is the study of how atoms join together to create every material we know.

HEALTH

Chemistry is important to many areas of life. For example, it keeps us healthy. Lots of medicines are developed each year using chemistry, and many tests are carried out in hospitals using chemicals.

 ## CHEMISTRY AT WORK

Chemistry is an important part of industry. New materials are developed all the time as a result of work carried out by chemists. Chemists are constantly working to find new, environmentally friendly fabrics, plastics, and more. Even some of our food is developed by chemists, such as new types of healthy food created from fungus.

There are lots of different types of chemistry, which can be broken down into five main branches or "disciplines."

 # ORGANIC CHEMISTRY

Organic chemistry is the study of chemicals that contain atoms of carbon. Most of the chemicals necessary for living things to flourish are carbon-based. Organic means "living."

 # INORGANIC CHEMISTRY

Inorganic chemistry is the study of chemicals that are not usually found in living things. These chemicals are often found in rocks or **minerals** dug from the ground. Currently, a lot of inorganic chemists are concentrating on the materials used for computers and for energy production.

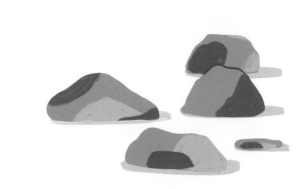

 # PHYSICAL CHEMISTRY

Physical chemistry studies how atoms bond together to create groups of atoms called **molecules**. A physical chemist might study **chemical reactions**, which is when the atoms in molecules are rearranged, creating new substances.

BIOCHEMISTRY

Biochemistry is the study of the chemical reactions that take place in living things—even you! Biochemists study the processes that take place in cells, and develop new treatments for diseases.

ANALYTICAL CHEMISTRY

Analytical chemistry is the study of the way matter is composed. It looks at how materials in samples of matter can be identified, separated, and quantified (finding out how much of a thing there is). Analytical chemists use a wide variety of complex instruments and experiments to find out about matter.

CHEMISTRY IS EVERYWHERE!

So—chemistry is going on all around us, every day—and lies behind lots of the things we take for granted in our lives, from computers to clothes and food!

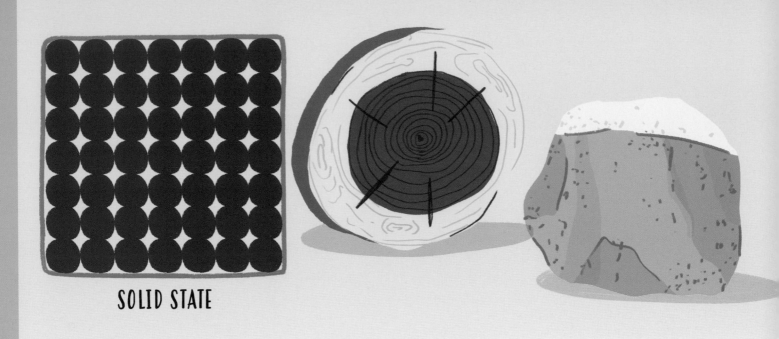

SOLID STATE

LIQUID STATE

GAS STATE

CHAPTER 1

STATES OF MATTER

There are four main common states (or "phases") of matter in the Universe:

| SOLID | LIQUID | GAS | PLASMA |

Matter is everything that has mass (or weight), and takes up space. Matter is made up of atoms and bonded groups of atoms, called molecules. Millions of them fit together to make all of the things we see and use every day—your home, trees, plants, and animals—even you are made of atoms!

SOLIDS

The ground you walk on is a solid; as are the chair you sit in; the plate you eat from; and a book you read—all solid things. Solids are "hard" things that you can hold.

GASES

The air you breathe is a gas. Molecules of gas are much farther apart than molecules in liquids. Gases are often invisible and we sometimes smell them rather than see them. Gases take on the shape and volume of the container they are held inside.

LIQUIDS

Liquids can be poured. They take on the shape of the containers they are put into. The juice you drink is liquid. Seawater, blood, milk, and water are all liquids.

PLASMA

We don't see plasma as often as solids, liquids, and gases. It is like a gas, but in this case some of the molecules have changed—they lose some of their electrons, and become ions. Plasma was only identified relatively recently in scientific terms—in 1879, by William Crookes.

CHANGING STATES

Sometimes, things change state. The molecules themselves don't change, but the way they move does. A water molecule is H_2O: two hydrogen atoms and one oxygen atom. That stays the same whether it is a liquid, solid (ice), or gas (steam). However, its physical state changes. Matter changes state when energy is applied, such as pressure or heat.

At room temperature, water is a liquid. The molecules can move about easily, so water drips and flows. It can change to a solid, as ice, when it freezes. In this form, the molecules are held together tightly and do not move easily. If we add heat energy, water can change into vapor called steam as it boils, like water in a kettle. The molecules move faster and spread far apart.

◆ SOLIDS ◆

How do we recognize when something is solid?
Ask yourself these questions:

- **DOES IT STAY IN ONE PLACE?**

- **DOES IT FLOW? IF IT DOES, IT IS NOT A SOLID.**

- **DOES IT HOLD ITS SHAPE? IF IT SPREADS OUT INTO THE AIR, IT IS NOT A SOLID.**

- **CAN IT BE SQUASHED OR COMPRESSED INTO A SMALL VOLUME? SOLIDS CAN'T CHANGE THE VOLUME THEY OCCUPY AS THE MOLECULES CAN'T MOVE CLOSER TOGETHER WITHOUT A CHANGE IN TEMPERATURE.**

Don't be fooled by powders such as salt or sand—they are still solids even though they can be "poured." Each tiny grain keeps the same shape and volume, so these are solids.

◆ SOLID STATE

Molecules vibrate as they have kinetic energy—they vibrate as they bump into each other. In a solid, forces keep the molecules tightly together and they vibrate (jiggle) in place. They don't move around past each other. The **electrons** move, but the atoms are locked into position.

Molecules in a solid are stuck in a rigid arrangement of atoms. They can't be compressed as there is nowhere for them to go. Strong forces bond the molecules, keeping them attracted to each other, keeping the solid together.

SOLID STATE

EXAMPLES OF SOLIDS

Solids can be lots of different textures—soft like fur and fabric or tough like stone and wood. Solid objects can be huge like cliffs at the coast or tiny like grains of sand.

SKIN

FUR

SAND GRAINS

FABRIC

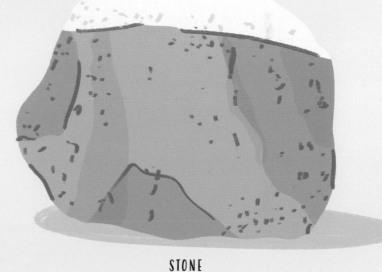

STONE

WOOD

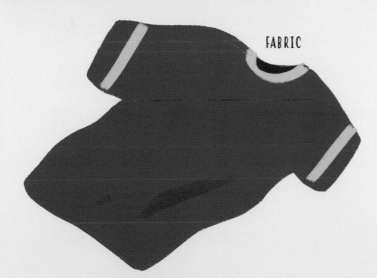

 # INTERMOLECULAR FORCES

All substances have forces that act to bring molecules together or apart— we call them intermolecular forces.

The molecules in solids are locked together. Liquids have cohesive (sticky) forces that pull molecules together, and molecules in gases spread out.

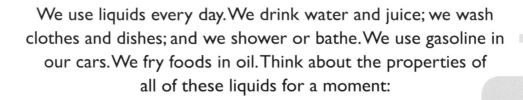

LIQUIDS

We use liquids every day. We drink water and juice; we wash clothes and dishes; and we shower or bathe. We use gasoline in our cars. We fry foods in oil. Think about the properties of all of these liquids for a moment:

- **THEY CAN BE POURED FROM ONE CONTAINER TO ANOTHER.**

- **THEY TAKE ON THE SHAPE OF THE CONTAINER THEY ARE IN.**

- **THEY CANNOT EASILY BE HELD IN YOUR HAND WITHOUT RUNNING THROUGH YOUR FINGERS.**

MOVEMENT

These properties that we can see are created by properties we cannot see. The molecules and atoms of liquids are free to move about, even though they are fairly close together. The particles are arranged in a random way and move around each other, so liquids flow. This is why liquids take on the shape of the container they are poured into.

Liquids have an almost fixed **volume** but no fixed shape. **Gravity** causes liquids to take on the shape of containers. Liquids cannot easily be compressed because the particles are close enough together that they have nowhere to move to.

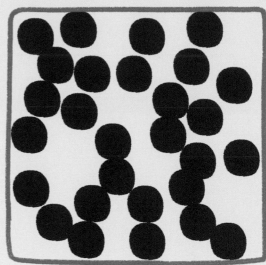

LIQUID STATE

VISCOSITY

Scientists talk about the viscosity of fluids. Water has low viscosity as it flows freely. Tar is a thick, sticky liquid that flows so slowly, it almost seems like a solid. It has high viscosity.

COHESIVE FORCES

Most liquids have strong cohesive (sticky) forces, which pull the molecules to keep them together. You can see that in action in your bathroom! When water drops onto a smooth surface such as a ceramic tile or glass, it makes a drop. It's the cohesive forces that stop the water molecules from spreading out.

The same force acts on a droplet of water dripping from a tap. It sticks together until it is too heavy and it falls—that's what makes that classic "drop of water" shape.

SURFACE TENSION

The same cohesive forces cause surface tension. It acts like a "skin" on the water, but there is no real skin—just forces at work. It happens because the forces at the surface work on the water molecules in a different way. In the main body of the liquid, the molecules are all pulled in every direction by the other molecules.

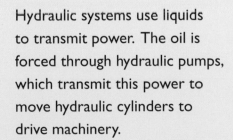

The molecules at the surface are pulled down and this squeezes them. The surface of the water seems to be elastic, like there was a skin. That's surface tension—and why pond skaters and water spiders can walk on water!

USES OF LIQUIDS

Liquids have lots of uses. They are used as solvents (to dissolve things). When things are dissolved in a liquid it is called a solution. Paints and most glues contain solvents. The solvents are very volatile, which means they disperse into the air easily—that's why we need to use them in well-ventilated spaces.

Liquids are also used as lubricants. They are used in engines, gear boxes, and machinery.

Hydraulic systems use liquids to transmit power. The oil is forced through hydraulic pumps, which transmit this power to move hydraulic cylinders to drive machinery.

Liquids are used as coolants. The fact that they flow means that they can be used to run through machines to remove excess heat. Water and glycol are used in engines for this purpose.

OUT OF CURIOSITY

There is even a liquid rock, called magma! It is found deep under the Earth. When it comes to the surface in a volcanic eruption, the flow is called lava.

Fridges, air conditioners, and heating systems use liquids to move heat from one place to another. Our bodies even use a liquid—sweat—to keep us cool as it evaporates.

GASES

Gas is all around us—the air we breathe is a gas!
The atmosphere is a layer of gases that surrounds Earth.

That hissing noise you hear when you open a can of soda? It's gas that has been held under pressure escaping. That's the same reason champagne corks make a pop sound when they come out of the neck of a bottle.

GAS STATE

 ## PLASMA

Plasma is found in stars and lightning. It is like a gas, but some of the molecules have changed—they lose some of their electrons, and become ions. Plasma is the most abundant state of matter in the universe!

USES OF GAS

Doctors use gas in hospitals—for example, to put people to sleep when they have operations (nitrous oxide). Divers also use gas tanks to breathe underwater (oxygen, nitrogen, helium).

FLOW

Gas particles are far apart, and randomly spaced. The attractive forces between the particles are weak, and they move quickly in all directions, independently of one another.

As a result, gas particles flow and completely fill a container, no matter how large it is. The particles spread out to fill the whole space equally.

HOW GAS MOVES

Have you ever seen smoke drifting above a fire? Or steam rising above a pan? They show us how gas moves. It flows like a liquid, and spreads or diffuses. That's why smoke and steam both seem to "disappear" into the air.

Gases have low density and low viscosity.

COMPRESSION

Gases can be compressed as the particles are far apart and have space to move into.

PRESSURE

When gas particles hit the side of a container, it creates pressure. If the temperature is increased, the particles move faster and hit the side more frequently, increasing pressure.

If the size of the container a gas is put into is decreased, the particles hit the side more often and this also increases the pressure. The weight of gas can create pressure on anything under it—on a planet, for example, this is called atmospheric pressure.

CHANGING STATE

Gases can change state, like other states of matter. If a temperature is low enough, gases can condense and turn into a liquid. If the temperature is low enough it can even change straight to a solid through a process called deposition. This process makes grass frosty in winter, when water in gas form is chilled and turns into solid ice.

OUT OF CURIOSITY
So what about vapor?
The word vapor describes gases that are usually liquid at room temperature—like water (H_2O). Water vapor, for example, is just water in its gaseous state.

MELTING POINT

The melting point of a substance is the temperature at which it changes from a solid state to a liquid one. Heat changes the state of the matter by affecting the bonds between particles.

 FLOW

When temperature rises, the molecules have more energy. They start to move faster, and soon have enough energy to break free from the solid structure, and flow as they move more easily. The substance has changed state, melting from a solid to a liquid.

 MELTING ICE

For pure water, the melting point of the solid state—ice—is 0° Celsius (or 32° Fahrenheit). If you add other substances to water, such as salt or sugar, the melting point lowers—that's why salt works on icy roads in winter.

DIFFERENT MELTING POINTS

Every element has a melting point—but some are much higher than others. Some substances are liquid at room temperature—this is around 18° Celsius (64.4°F). Olive oil, for example, is liquid at room temperature.

The element gallium (Ga) is a soft, silvery metal used in the manufacture of electronics. It melts at a low temperature—around 29° Celsius (84°F)—so it could melt from the heat of your hand!

MELTING AND FREEZING POINTS

An interesting point to note is that the melting point of a solid is the same as the freezing point of the substance in its liquid form. It makes sense, if you think about it!

MELTING POINTS:

WATER (H_2O): 0° CELSIUS (32°F)

CHOCOLATE: 35° CELSIUS (95°F)

PHOSPHORUS (P): 44° CELSIUS (111°F)

BEESWAX: 64° CELSIUS (147°F)

LEAD (PB): 327° CELSIUS (620°F)

IRON (FE): 1,538° CELSIUS (2,800°F)

BOILING POINT

The boiling point is the temperature at which a substance boils— which means it reaches a state of rapid evaporation, changing state from a liquid to a gas. When a liquid becomes a gas we call the process vaporization. The molecules have been heated to such a point that they vibrate quickly and bonds between them are weakened until they break free to become a gas.

WATER

For pure water, boiling point (bp) is 100° Celsius (212°F). Have you ever watched a kettle boil and seen steam come out of the spout? The kettle turns off when the water reaches boiling point—and we have to be very careful or we can get scalded.

AIR PRESSURE

Amazingly, the boiling point of a liquid depends on the pressure of the surrounding air. High air pressure increases the boiling point, whereas low air pressure makes the boiling point drop. At the top of a high mountain, such as K2 or Mount Everest, there is lower air pressure. The top of Mount Everest is 8,848 m (29,029 ft) above sea level. The air is so "thin" and the air pressure so much lower than at sea level, that water boils at a lower temperature, at about 70° Celsius (156°F). Celebrating the climb with a "quick" cup of tea or coffee takes on a new meaning!

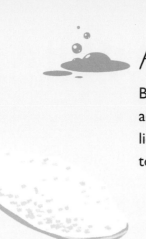

ADDING SUBSTANCES

Boiling points can be changed by the addition of other substances to the liquid. For example, adding salt or sugar to water changes its boiling point.

OUT OF CURIOSITY

Evaporation is what happens when a liquid becomes a gas—but only at the surface of the liquid. It does not need a high temperature or boiling point for that to occur. Think about a puddle on the ground. The molecules at the surface are in contact with the air and on a sunny day the puddle dries quickly. As it does so, the liquid water has become water vapor.

BROWNIAN MOTION

Brownian motion is the name given to the random motion of particles in liquids and gases. It is caused by the fast-moving atoms or molecules in liquids and gases, and was discovered by (and named for) the botanist Robert Brown, who discovered the phenomenon in 1827. He was studying the life cycle of a newly discovered plant.

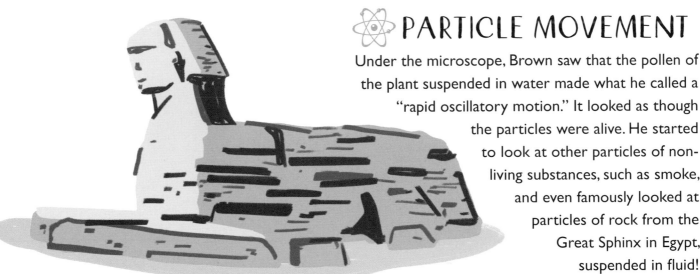

PARTICLE MOVEMENT

Under the microscope, Brown saw that the pollen of the plant suspended in water made what he called a "rapid oscillatory motion." It looked as though the particles were alive. He started to look at other particles of non-living substances, such as smoke, and even famously looked at particles of rock from the Great Sphinx in Egypt, suspended in fluid!

BOMBARDMENT

In 1905, physicist Albert Einstein produced his theory of Brownian motion. He explained that particles in liquids and gases move randomly because they are being bombarded constantly by other moving particles.

Einstein said that pollen grains moved in water because they were being moved by individual water molecules—proving that atoms and molecules did in fact exist.

⚛ DISPERSAL

Brownian motion is responsible for the way smells disperse or diffuse. The motion jostles the particles and the smell spreads into the air around it—pee-yew!

⚛ NANOTECHNOLOGY

Researchers in recent years have been looking at ways to harness Brownian motion in **nanotechnology**.

Scientists in Japan have demonstrated that Brownian motion can be used to convert information into energy. They hope that this will one day lead to smart devices, such as phones, that can power themselves.

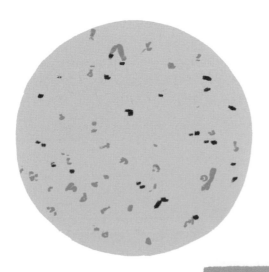

⊙ ELEMENTS ⊙

A chemical element is a substance that contains one type of atom
(if a substance has more than one type of atom, it is a compound).
An element is any substance that cannot be broken down by
ordinary chemical processes into simpler substances.

Elements are the building blocks of all substances, and can be in any state of
matter—solid, liquid, or gas—but most are solids at room temperature. There are only 11
elements that are gases at room temperature (the noble gases plus hydrogen (H), oxygen (O),
nitrogen (N), fluorine (F), chlorine (CL)) and two liquids (bromine (Br) and mercury (Hg)).

⊙ NUMBER OF ELEMENTS

There are 118 chemical elements known to chemistry today.
Only 92 of these are found in nature, the last of which to be
discovered was uranium (U), discovered in 1789. The rest are made in
laboratories. The first element made in this way was technetium (Tc) in 1937.

⊙ THE PERIODIC TABLE

Scientists have arranged the chemical elements on the periodic table. Their position tells
us about their properties. They have chemical symbols which are used across the world.
That means that scientists use the same symbol, wherever they are located, and whichever
language they speak! The symbols come largely from their Latin names.

GOLD – symbol Au from Latin for gold: *aurum*

SILVER – symbol Ag from Latin for silver: *argentum*

LEAD – symbol Pb from Latin: *plumbum*

SODIUM – symbol Na from Latin: *natrium*

1 H																	2 He
3 Li	4 Be											5 B	6 C	7 N	8 O	9 F	10 Ne
11 Na	12 Mg											13 Al	14 Si	15 P	16 S	17 Cl	18 Ar
19 K	20 Ca	21 Sc	22 Ti	23 V	24 Cr	25 Mn	26 Fe	27 Co	28 Ni	29 Cu	30 Zn	31 Ga	32 Ge	33 As	34 Se	35 Br	36 Kr
37 Rb	38 Sr	39 Y	40 Zr	41 Nb	42 Mo	43 Tc	44 Ru	45 Rh	46 Pd	47 Ag	48 Cd	49 In	50 Sn	51 Sb	52 Te	53 I	54 Xe
55 Cs	56 Ba	57-71	72 Hf	73 Ta	74 W	75 Re	76 Os	77 Ir	78 Pt	79 Au	80 Hg	81 Tl	82 Pb	83 Bi	84 Po	85 At	86 Rn
87 Fr	88 Ra	89-103	104 Rf	105 Db	106 Sg	107 Bh	108 Hs	109 Mt	110 Ds	111 Rg	112 Cn	113 Nh	114 Fl	115 Mc	116 Lv	117 Ts	118 Og

57 La	58 Ce	59 Pr	60 Nd	61 Pm	62 Sm	63 Eu	64 Gd	65 Tb	66 Dy	67 Ho	68 Er	69 Tm	70 Yb	71 Lu
89 Ac	90 Th	91 Pa	92 U	93 Np	94 Pu	95 Am	96 Cm	97 Bk	98 Cf	99 Es	100 Fm	101 Md	102 No	103 Lr

⊚ ATOMIC NUMBERS

The atomic number of an element is the number of **protons** in each atom. The atomic number of an element affects its position on the periodic table. Hydrogen (H) is the first element and has the atomic number 1 because it has one proton. Gold (Au) has the atomic number 79 because it has 79 protons in each atom.

⊚ PROPERTIES

On the periodic table, elements are grouped together in families according to their specific properties. Noble gases are one family. Helium (He), xenon (Xe), neon (Ne), radon (Rn), and argon (Ar) are all classed as noble gases.

⊚ EARLY IDEAS

For 2,000 years, starting from about 450 BCE, people in Europe believed the elements were Earth, Air, Fire, and Water. In the Middle Ages, **alchemists** added two new elements of a different kind, sulfur (which meant combustibility to them), and mercury (which meant volatility). A third, salt (solidity), was added in the 1500s.

❓ OUT OF CURIOSITY

Hydrogen (H) is the lightest element—and it is the most abundant element in the Universe.

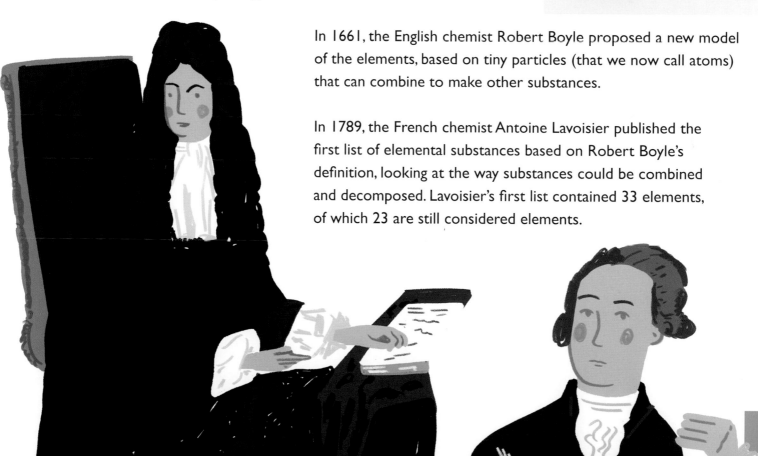

In 1661, the English chemist Robert Boyle proposed a new model of the elements, based on tiny particles (that we now call atoms) that can combine to make other substances.

In 1789, the French chemist Antoine Lavoisier published the first list of elemental substances based on Robert Boyle's definition, looking at the way substances could be combined and decomposed. Lavoisier's first list contained 33 elements, of which 23 are still considered elements.

COMPOUNDS

A chemical compound is a chemical formed from the atoms of different chemical elements.

The atoms are bonded together and the chemical compound behaves like a single substance with properties of its own—which may be different than the properties of the elements it is made from! Salt, or sodium chloride, is a perfect example.

SALT

Sodium chloride (NaCl) is made up of one atom of sodium and one atom of chlorine. Now, sodium (Na) is a metal that burns in the presence of water, and chlorine (Cl) is a poisonous gas—but put together in equal proportions, they make the salt we use to safely season our food!

WATER

Water (H_2O) is also a compound. It is made up of hydrogen and oxygen atoms. There are two hydrogen (H) atoms and one oxygen (O) atom.

COMPOUNDS ALL AROUND

There are a huge number of compounds—maybe as many as 61 million! More compounds are discovered by scientists working in laboratories every day. Compounds can even be made by combining other compounds to create new chemicals.

The chemical reaction that takes place when a substance is heated, for example, may join atoms together to create a new compound or even several new compounds. The possibilities are exciting and seemingly endless.

RESEARCH

Chemists work to find new medicines, cleaning materials, glue, and more—and businesses employ scientists to research and develop these new compounds to make their products work better.

BONDS

Once compounds have been made, they can be hard to break down. They are not like mixtures, which are just physically combined and can be easily separated again. Chemical bonds are created when compounds are made. They have combined to make a completely new substance.

MIXTURES

In chemistry, a mixture is a substance containing two or more elements or chemical compounds. Mixtures can be solids, liquids, or gases. Mixtures are different from compounds because the combined substances do not chemically react to form new molecular bonds. Each component or part of the mixture keeps its original properties.

Mixtures can be separated into their component parts by physical processes such as **filtration, evaporation,** and **distillation** (see pages 94-97). Seawater, for example, can be separated by evaporation into its two main components, which are water (H_2O) and salt or sodium chloride ($NaCl$). There are also other compounds in seawater.

SEAWATER

Seawater is an example of a solution. This is created when one substance dissolves into another.

Another example would be sugar being stirred into hot water until it dissolves.

SOLUTIONS

Solutions combine a solute (the substance that dissolves) and a solvent (the thing the solute is dissolved by).

Solutions are known as homogenous mixtures. This means all of the substances are evenly distributed (spread) through the mixture. In seawater, the salt is the solute and the water is the solvent.

SUSPENSIONS

Other mixtures are suspensions. Muddy water is a suspension of soil in water. The soil does not dissolve; it merely floats in the water.

Sand in water is a heterogenous mixture, which means that there is not an even distribution of substances throughout.

If you stir a heterogenous mixture and leave it to settle, some of the solids will sink to the bottom of the container. These particles could be removed by filtration.

MIXTURES

Solids can also be mixtures. Most soils and rocks are mixtures of different materials.

Liquids can also be mixtures, such as salad dressing that combines oil and other liquids to create an emulsion. Over time, these settle and separate, and we shake them before we use them to mix them up again.

MIXED GASES

Gases can be mixtures too, such as the air we breathe, which is a mixture of nitrogen, oxygen, and other gases.

It is much more difficult to separate gases mixed together as the particles are too small to separate by physical means. One method is to find a solvent that will dissolve one of the gases, and remove the gas from the solution by itself.

COLLOIDS

Do you like to drink milk or put it on your cereal? Believe it or not, milk is a mixture. It is an example of a colloid. That is a heterogenous type of mixture. Tiny particles of liquid butterfat are suspended in water. Particles in colloids do not sink to the bottom over time, but stay suspended.

ALLOYS

Alloys are mixtures of different metals. The combined metals have different properties from separate metals. For example, nickel (Ni) or chromium (Cr) might be added to steel to help it to resist rust.

CHAPTER 2

CHEMICAL BUILDING BLOCKS

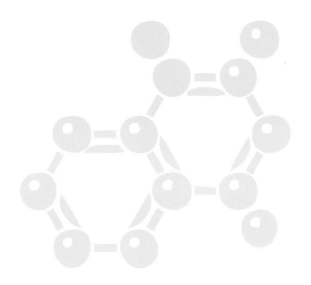

We live in a Universe made up of "matter."
That means any substance that has mass
(measured in kilograms or pounds) and takes
up space by having volume (size).

Matter is made up of tiny particles called atoms and
molecules. These microscopic things combine to make up
everything. Atoms are like building blocks that fit together
to make different substances. Molecules are made up of
two or more atoms that are held together by chemical
bonds. Polymers are big molecules, made up of smaller
molecules joined together.

MORE THAN ATOMS

When scientists first began to understand atoms in the
early 20th century, they thought they were about to
understand the basis of all matter—but they were wrong.

Swiss astronomer Fritz Zwicky began to argue that parts
of the Universe had to be made of other things entirely
in the 1930s.

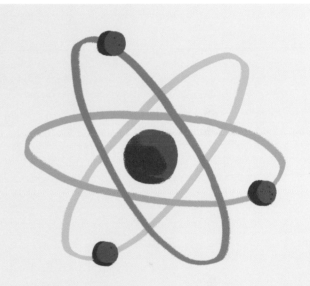

DARK MATTER

Scientists think that the Universe also contains a
different form of matter, called dark matter. Dark
matter cannot be seen directly; it does not absorb,
reflect, or give off light. No wonder it is called "dark"
matter! Scientists are still finding out about dark
matter and how it works.

Normal matter
is not boring just
because it is "normal"!

Tiny atoms are part
of everything you can
see and touch. Isn't
that amazing?

ATOMS

Atoms are the building blocks that join together to make all of the ordinary matter in the Universe. They are incredibly small—smaller than a pinprick. You can only see them with an incredibly powerful microscope. There are about 7 billion billion billion atoms in a human, which is octillions!

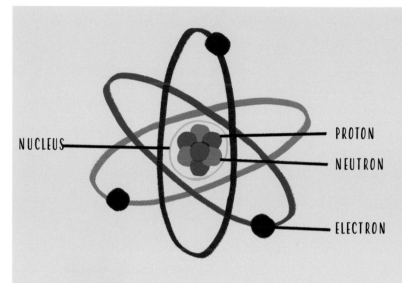

Atoms are made up of even smaller particles. These are electrons, protons, and neutrons.

In the middle of an atom is the nucleus, made up of positively charged protons and neutral neutrons. The negatively charged electrons are attracted or pulled toward the protons because they have the opposite charge. They spin around the nucleus in tiny orbits, like a satellite orbiting Earth.

THE PERIODIC

1 H								
3 Li	4 Be							
11 Na	12 Mg							
19 K	20 Ca	21 Sc	22 Ti	23 V	24 Cr	25 Mn	26 Fe	27 Co
37 Rb	38 Sr	39 Y	40 Zr	41 Nb	42 Mo	43 Tc	44 Ru	45 Rh
55 Cs	56 Ba	57-71	72 Hf	73 Ta	74 W	75 Re	76 Os	77 Ir
87 Fr	88 Ra	89-103	104 Rf	105 Db	106 Sg	107 Bh	108 Hs	109 Mt

57 La	58 Ce	59 Pr	60 Nd	61 Pm	62 Sm	63 Eu
89 Ac	90 Th	91 Pa	92 U	93 Np	94 Pu	95 Am

Each element is a different type of atom. The number of protons an atom contains decides what kind of element it is. That gives the element its "atomic number."

The **periodic table** is arranged in atomic number order—take a look! An atom with one proton in the nucleus is hydrogen (H). An atom with two protons is helium (He). Can you find them on the periodic table?

In chemistry, we look at the way the electrons in an element pair up or share with other atoms. Sometimes, they even shift to other atoms completely, and create ions—an atom or molecule with an electric charge.

TABLE

					2 He
5 B	6 C	7 N	8 O	9 F	10 Ne
13 Al	14 Si	15 P	16 S	17 Cl	18 Ar

28 Ni	29 Cu	30 Zn	31 Ga	32 Ge	33 As	34 Se	35 Br	36 Kr
46 Pd	47 Ag	48 Cd	49 In	50 Sn	51 Sb	52 Te	53 I	54 Xe
78 Pt	79 Au	80 Hg	81 Tl	82 Pb	83 Bi	84 Po	85 At	86 Rn
110 Ds	111 Rg	112 Cn	113 Nh	114 Fl	115 Mc	116 Lv	117 Ts	118 Og

64 Gd	65 Tb	66 Dy	67 Ho	68 Er	69 Tm	70 Yb	71 Lu
96 Cm	97 Bk	98 Cf	99 Es	100 Fm	101 Md	102 No	103 Lr

MOLECULES

Molecules are two or more atoms held together by a chemical bond. A molecule is the smallest "unit" of a substance that has the properties of the substance.

The chemical name for water is H_2O. That means there are two hydrogen atoms and one oxygen atom in each molecule of water. The atoms do not make water until they are chemically bonded—just mixing the two gases together doesn't make water vapor.

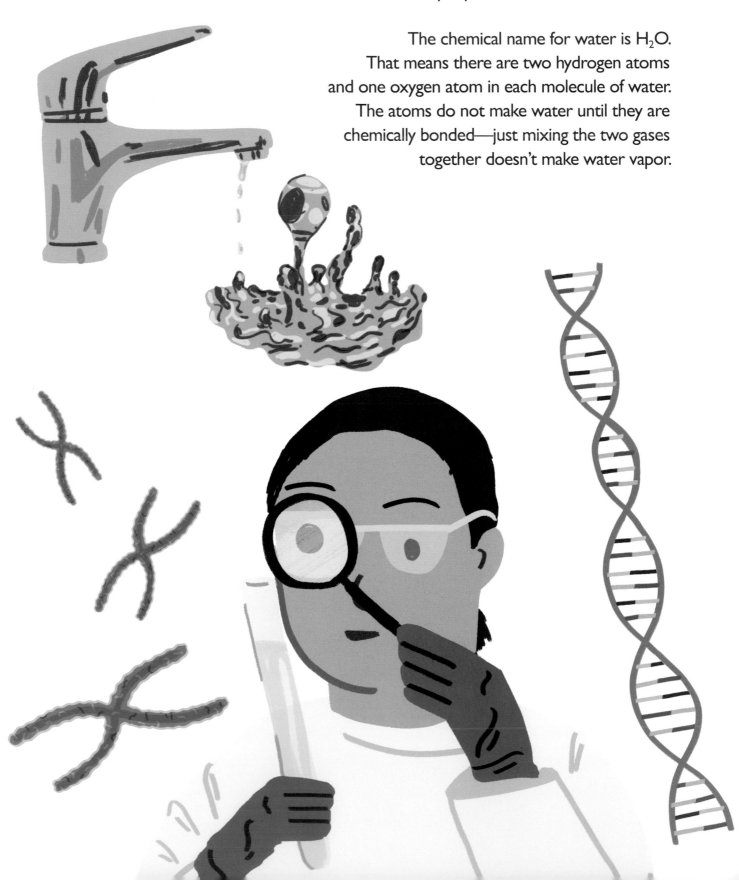

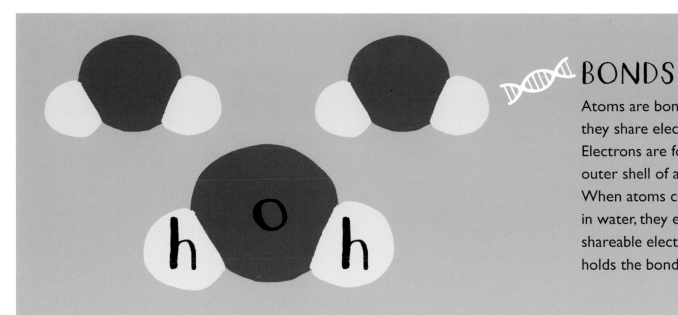

BONDS

Atoms are bonded when they share electrons. Electrons are found in the outer shell of an atom. When atoms combine, as in water, they each share shareable electrons. This holds the bond together.

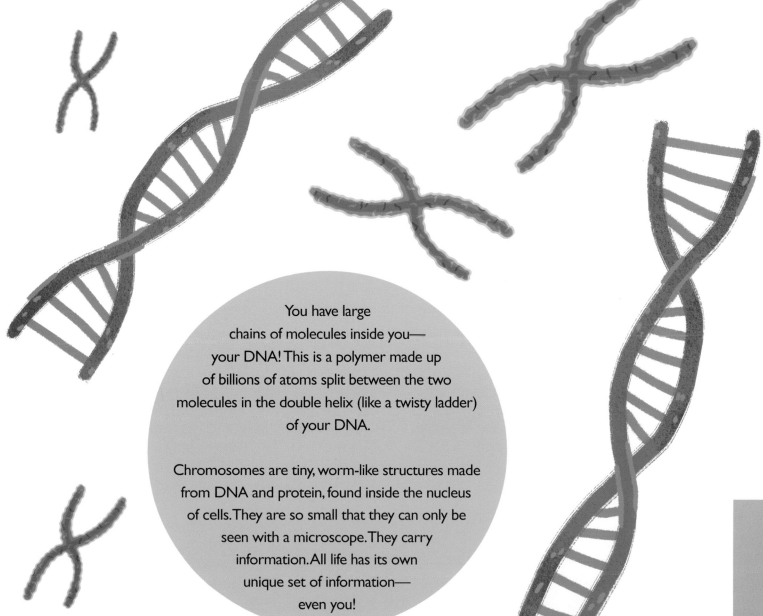

You have large chains of molecules inside you—your DNA! This is a polymer made up of billions of atoms split between the two molecules in the double helix (like a twisty ladder) of your DNA.

Chromosomes are tiny, worm-like structures made from DNA and protein, found inside the nucleus of cells. They are so small that they can only be seen with a microscope. They carry information. All life has its own unique set of information—even you!

POLYMERS

Have you drunk from a plastic bottle today? Or used a plastic bag for shopping?
Have you worn nylon fleece or a raincoat? Or maybe written on a piece of paper?
If so, you have used a **polymer**!

Some polymers are found in nature. Cellulose is a
strong polymer found in the cell walls of plants that
helps them to stand up. Wood, paper, and cotton
all contain cellulose. Cellulose is what makes fibers
in plants, like hemp and cotton. It is the strength of
these natural polymers that allows us to twist fibers
into strong thread that can be used to make fabric.

Cellulose is the fiber in our foods,
such as vegetables. We cannot
digest fiber, but it helps us to keep
our digestive systems healthy.

ARTIFICIAL POLYMERS

Artificial polymers are big molecules made up of smaller molecules (called **monomers**) laid out in a repeating pattern.

Some plastics are made from crude oil that has been extracted from the ground. It is refined and broken down into monomers which are then used to create the polymers for plastic.

The polymers can be created to form hard, rigid, flexible, or soft plastic, depending on how they are made.

AMAZING AMBER

Amber is fossilized tree resin and a natural polymer. It started as sticky sap and hardened over time. That means amber can be found with ancient insects trapped inside—just like the mosquito in the film, *Jurassic Park*.

In the movie, fictional scientists extracted dinosaur blood and the all-important DNA that started everything—not that that would be possible in real life!

# ⚛ ISOTOPES ⚛

Isotopes are atoms of an element with the same number of protons, but a different number of neutrons—sometimes more and sometimes less. This makes them less stable than normal atoms. An atom of a radioisotope gives off energy or particles. It may change the number of protons it has and so "decay" into a different element. Being exposed to this energy, called radiation, is usually thought of as being harmful to the human body, but radioactive decay can make isotopes useful in medicine.

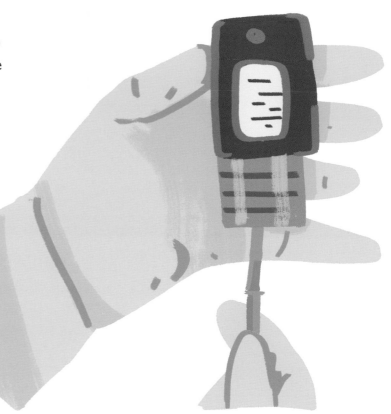

For example, doctors use barium isotopes to trace food as it passes through the gut, as the barium appears white in x-rays. This can help them to diagnose and treat health problems.

Technetium-99m is used as a tracer. It can be injected or inhaled by the patient. It then travels through the body and the radiation it gives off can be tracked. Doctors can look at images and see organ function and bone growth.

Radioisotopes used in this way decay quickly, before they can cause any harm to the patient's body.

 ## RADIOTHERAPY

Radiotherapy uses radioisotopes to treat cancer. This disrupts the molecules of the tissue treated, and causes breaks in the DNA molecule. This kills cancer cells. It can cause unpleasant side effects that make patients feel ill, but it is an important tool in the fight against cancer.

 # DANGER!

Isotopes can also be dangerous. Plutonium-239 and Uranium-235 are used to make nuclear weapons—perhaps the most destructive and deadliest weapons in the world.

Nuclear fission happens when a single free neutron strikes the nucleus of an atom of radioactive materials such as plutonium or uranium. When this happens, it bumps into two to three more neutrons, which split off from the nucleus, releasing energy. The freed neutrons strike other nuclei and set off a chain reaction. More and more energy is released with terrible effects.

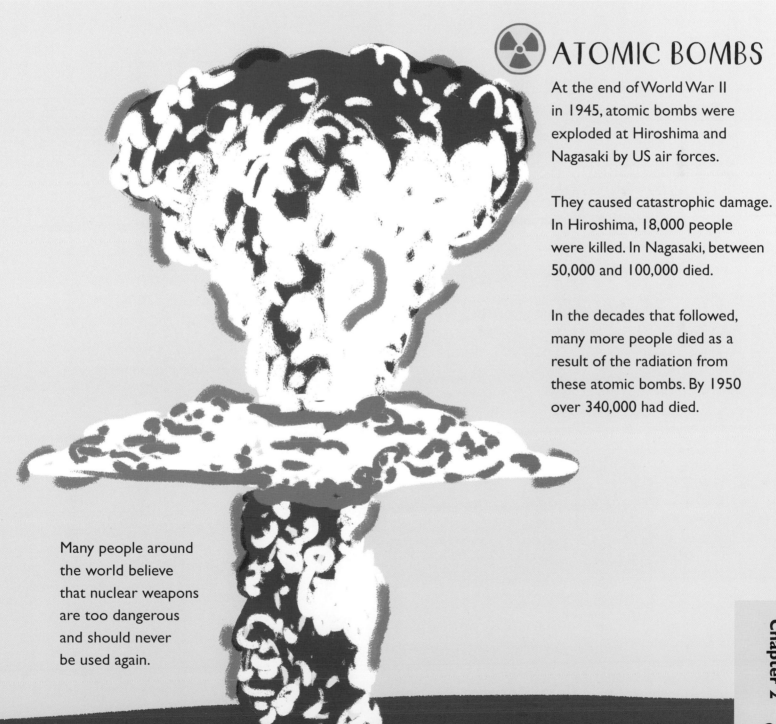

ATOMIC BOMBS

At the end of World War II in 1945, atomic bombs were exploded at Hiroshima and Nagasaki by US air forces.

They caused catastrophic damage. In Hiroshima, 18,000 people were killed. In Nagasaki, between 50,000 and 100,000 died.

In the decades that followed, many more people died as a result of the radiation from these atomic bombs. By 1950 over 340,000 had died.

Many people around the world believe that nuclear weapons are too dangerous and should never be used again.

NANOPARTICLES

Nanotechnology is a part of science that deals with things on an atomic or molecular scale. That means things that are 100 nanometers or less in size. One nanometer (nm) is 0.000000001 meters. "Nano" means "billionth," so a nanometer is a billionth of a meter. To give an idea of just how small that is, it is about 1/25,000th of the diameter of a human hair. Your fingernails grow a nanometer per second—amazing!

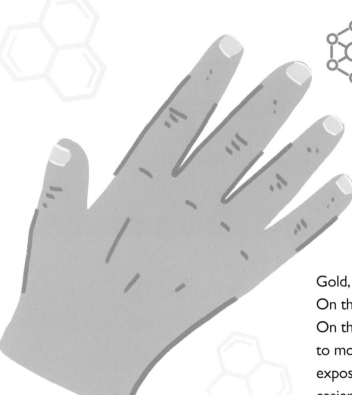

TINY MOVEMENTS

Nanoparticles are tiny. We can only see them with a special electron microscope. They may be small—but they can be incredibly useful! Nanoparticles of an element often behave differently from larger particles of the same material.

Gold, for example, is usually not very **reactive**. On the nanoscale, it becomes very chemically active. On the nanoscale, it is easier for atoms and molecules to move around. They have much more surface area exposed to other nanoparticles and this makes it easier for chemical reactions to take place.

EVERYDAY NANOPARTICLES

Nanoparticles are used in many areas of everyday life. Sunscreen often contains nanoparticles of zinc or titanium oxide to block the sun's ultraviolet (UV) rays—so they save you from sunburn! Cosmetics also can contain nanoparticles.

NANOWHISKERS

Some materials contain "nanowhiskers"—tiny fibers that coat the fabric and keep it clean.

Nanowhiskers can be used to help to make things like car bumpers scratch resistant, and paint that is corrosion resistant.

DRESSING IN SILVER

Nanoparticles such as colloidal silver are also used in some dressings to care for wounds, to keep them clean and free from infection.

pH

Scientists use a **pH** (power of hydrogen) scale to measure how acidic or basic a solution is. A pH scale is numbered from 0 to 14. Low numbers from 0–7 are acids. The lower the number, the more acidic the liquid is. Battery acid from a car would have a pH of 0, and lemon juice would be about 2.

TESTING ... TESTING ...

pH can only be tested when a solution is aqueous—that means, it is in water. Some liquids such as vegetable oil or pure alcohol have no pH value at all.

BASE

Liquids numbered from 7—14 are bases. The higher the number, the stronger the base. Liquid drain cleaner would have a pH of 14, and bleach would be 13.

LITMUS TEST

There are lots of ways to measure the pH of a liquid. Litmus paper is cheap and easy to use. When you touch a piece of the paper to a liquid, it changes its shade to show if the liquid is an acid or base. If the paper goes red, then the liquid is acidic, but if the paper turns blue, it is basic.

NEUTRAL

If the pH is 7, the liquid is neutral. That would be a liquid such as distilled water.

DISTILLED WATER

OUT OF CURIOSITY

A healthy person's blood has a pH of around 7.4—quite neutral!

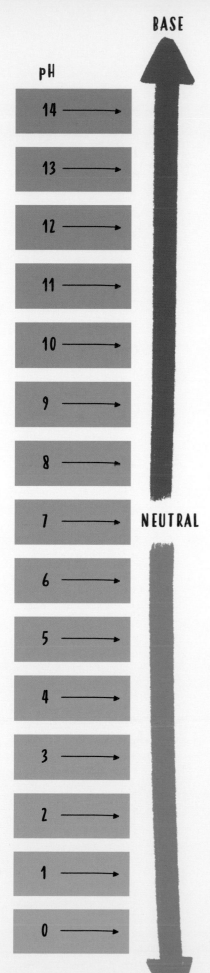

EXAMPLES

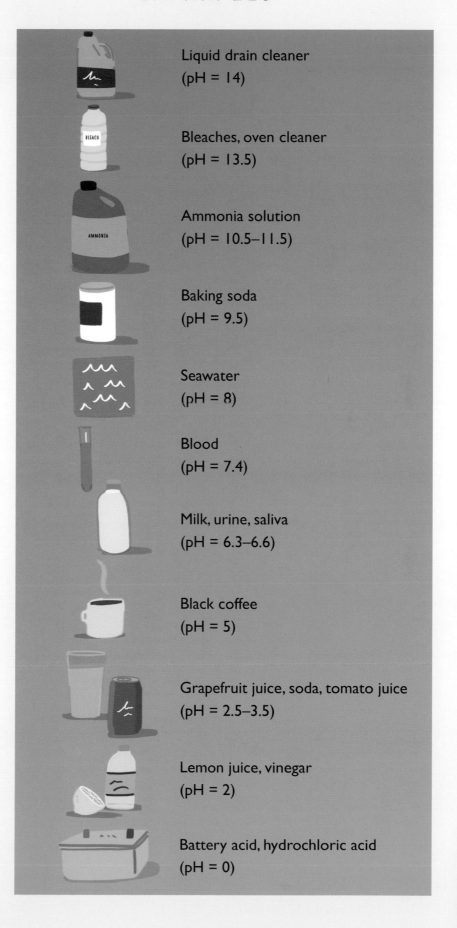

Liquid drain cleaner
(pH = 14)

Bleaches, oven cleaner
(pH = 13.5)

Ammonia solution
(pH = 10.5–11.5)

Baking soda
(pH = 9.5)

Seawater
(pH = 8)

Blood
(pH = 7.4)

Milk, urine, saliva
(pH = 6.3–6.6)

Black coffee
(pH = 5)

Grapefruit juice, soda, tomato juice
(pH = 2.5–3.5)

Lemon juice, vinegar
(pH = 2)

Battery acid, hydrochloric acid
(pH = 0)

 # ACIDS

Acids are chemicals with a low pH. Acids have a pH lower than 7. Always be careful around acids as they can be very dangerous! Strong acid can burn skin badly.

 ## POWER OF HYDROGEN

All acids contain hydrogen. That's why pH contains hydrogen's symbol— the letter "H." When they are dissolved in water, acids lose some of their hydrogen in the form of electrically charged atoms, or ions. Strong acids (with a pH of 1–3) lose all of their positive hydrogen ions instantly, and those ions may bond with other chemicals in powerful reactions. Weaker acids (pH 4–6) hold on to some of their ions. The amount of ions that an acid releases tell us its *power*—which gives us the "p" in pH!

DANGER!

Always remember that acids can be very dangerous, so check with an adult first and never touch anything marked with a warning sign.

 ## ACIDS:

- Can sting the skin or damage it
- Turn litmus paper red
- Conduct electricity (acid is used in batteries)
- Can corrode metal
- Contain hydrogen

OUT OF CURIOSITY

You even have some acids in your body! Your DNA is a type of acid, called a nucleic acid. You also have hydrochloric acid in your digestive system, to help you to digest food.

KEEP AWAY!

Some creatures produce acid as a defense! Ants produce formic acid, and some octopi produce magneta, a black inky acid.

BATTERIES CONTAIN SULFURIC ACID

CITRUS FRUITS CONTAIN CITRIC ACID

YOGURT CONTAINS LACTIC ACID

VINEGAR CONTAINS ACETIC ACID

BASES AND ALKALIS

A base is the "chemical opposite" to an acid. It is a substance that can accept a hydrogen ion from another substance. Some bases are weak and others are strong. An **alkali** is any solution with a pH of more than 7. It is created when a base is dissolved in water. It can be neutralized, or brought down to a pH of 7, by adding an acid to the mix.

DANGER!

Alkalis can be very dangerous and burn your skin. Never touch any chemicals without an adult present and using proper skin and eye protection.

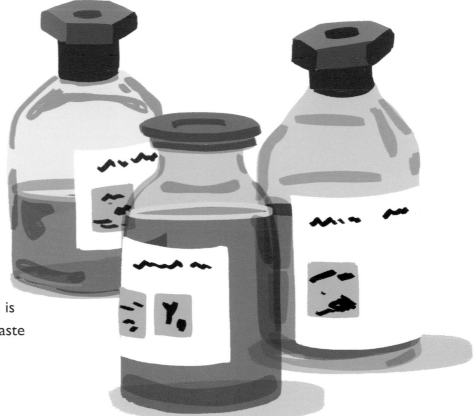

 ALKALIS:

- Feel "soapy"
- The higher the number on the pH scale, the stronger the alkali is
- Edible alkalis can have a bitter taste
- Are easily dissolved in water
- Turn litmus paper blue
- Can conduct electricity

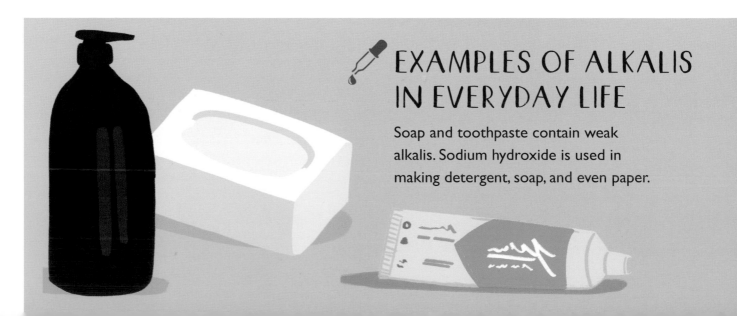

EXAMPLES OF ALKALIS IN EVERYDAY LIFE

Soap and toothpaste contain weak alkalis. Sodium hydroxide is used in making detergent, soap, and even paper.

 ## HELPFUL ALKALIS

Potassium hydroxide is used to make soil less acidic so plants will grow. Magnesium hydroxide is used as an indigestion remedy to make stomach contents less acidic.

BLEACH

Some heavy-duty cleaning products like bleach and drain cleaner contain strong alkalis and they can damage your skin.

OUT OF CURIOSITY

The word "alkali" comes from the Arabic word "*quali*" which means "from the ashes." Ashes were used in traditional soap making—and most cleaning products are alkali!

BUILDING BLOCKS

Calcium carbonate is used in building. It is chalk lime, used in some mortar and cement, and also makes up stones called marble and limestone.

⚗ UNIVERSAL INDICATOR ⚗

Universal indicator (UI) can be used to find out the pH of a liquid. UI is used either as a strip of paper, or as a liquid. It shows pH values precisely, from 0–14. UI is made from a clever mixture of different substances that change their shade at different pH values.

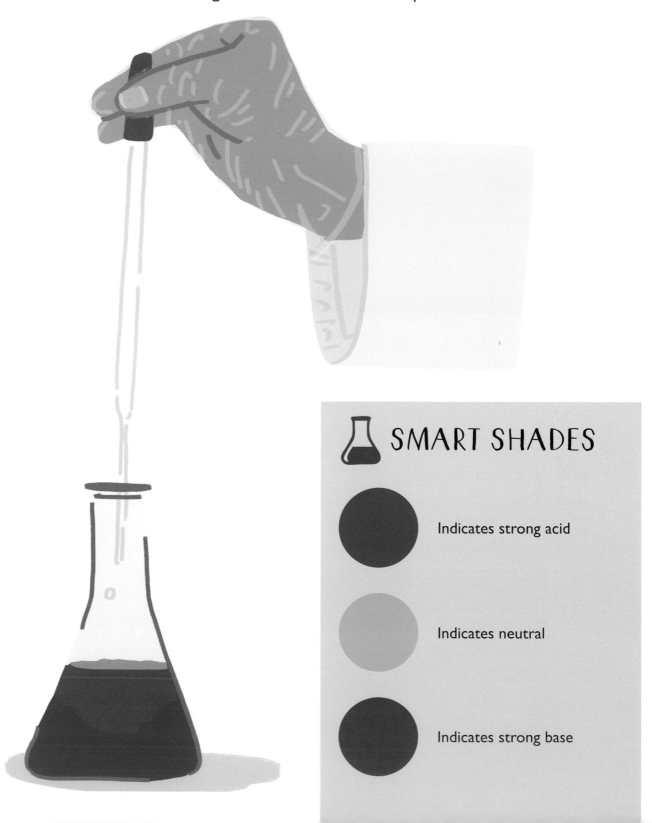

⚗ SMART SHADES

Indicates strong acid

Indicates neutral

Indicates strong base

 KEYS

When you buy commercial universal indicator paper or solution, it comes with a special key to tell you what each shade means. This chart is used by comparing the shade of the paper or solution used against the key. Then you can "read" the result.

OUT OF CURIOSITY

The pigment found in red cabbage juice is a naturally occurring universal indicator! You can easily make some yourself and use it to test drinks in the kitchen and hand soap in the bathroom to find their pH value.

Chop up red cabbage and boil it for a few minutes. Wait until it is completely cool and strain off the liquid. You can put the liquid in containers and add drops of different, but safe-to-use liquids, to test their pH.

RED CABBAGE UNIVERSAL INDICATOR

0 1 2 3 4 5 6 7 8 9 10 11 12 13 14

← ACIDIC ——— pH ——— ALKALINE →

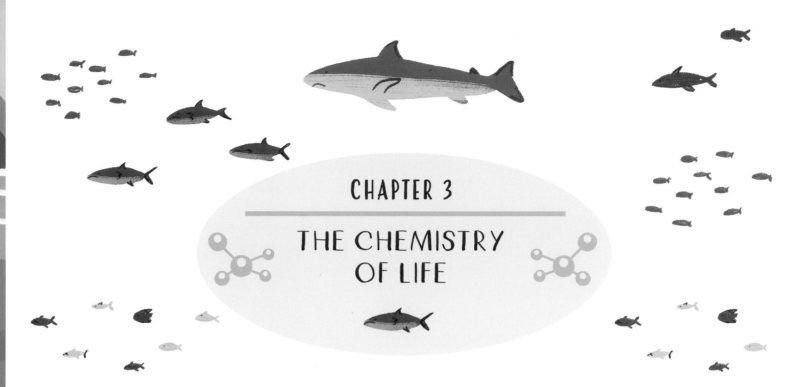

CHAPTER 3

THE CHEMISTRY OF LIFE

All living things use chemicals and chemical reactions to live. Plants, humans, and other animals—we all need chemicals and chemical processes to function. All life is carbon-based, which means it contains carbon atoms. There's a lot of carbon stored out there in trees, plants, your cat—and even you! Carbon is the fourth most common type of atom in the whole universe.

Other chemicals are also widely used by living things, including hydrogen, oxygen, and nitrogen. Sulfur and phosphorous are also key building blocks for all living things. Living **organisms** have processes that use these chemicals to form molecules such as carbohydrates and proteins that we need to live, grow, and be healthy.

WATER

Most of the Earth is covered by water—that's why it looks so blue from space. An amazing 71% of the surface of the Earth is covered by oceans, lakes, and rivers.

Water is transparent, tasteless, and smell free. This might make it sound less than exciting—but if you have ever seen a roaring river, a pounding waterfall, or stormy seas, you know it is anything but! Water is everywhere, in the form of a liquid, gas, and solid. Drops of liquid water fall as rain. Water vapor is an invisible gas that floats in the air. Water freezes into solid ice at the North and South Poles.

WATER FOR HEALTH

Without water, there would be no life on Earth, as all living things need water to survive. You are made up of around 60% water. If you don't drink enough, you soon feel tired and grumpy, and even become ill.

Water carries essential materials around the body. Many of the chemical processes that happen in your body require water, and if you get **dehydrated** they don't work properly. That's bad news for you and your health!

Have you ever seen a plant wilting? They cannot function correctly without water, so the plant droops and will eventually dry out and die.

COOL, COOL WATER

Water is useful for regulating temperatures on Earth, too. The oceans store heat from the Sun, which affects global temperatures and weather systems. Water also cools humans down. When we get too hot, we sweat. Sweat is 90% water. As the sweat evaporates, or turns to invisible gas, we cool down. This is because it takes heat to evaporate the sweat, and that heat comes from our body.

WHAT MAKES WATER?

Water is made of tiny molecules, each of them made of one atom of oxygen and two atoms of hydrogen that are bonded together. Hydrogen is the lightest and most common type of atom in the Universe. Oxygen is the third most common type of atom. It easily joins with other atoms to form molecules.

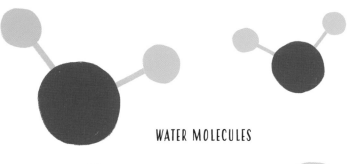

WATER MOLECULES

OUT OF CURIOSITY

When water gets very cold, it changes state from a liquid to a solid—ice. You will be familiar with that if you have seen frozen puddles on a wintry day or you have enjoyed ice pops and ice cream. But did you know that ice is less dense than water? That's why it floats! **Density** is a measure of how tightly packed the molecules in a substance are. Materials that are less dense than water—like ice and foam swimming floats—will float on water.

OXYGEN

O₂

Without oxygen we could not live on Earth! From the tiniest beetle to the biggest whale, almost all living things—including us—need oxygen to live. Without it, we could not breathe.

THE OXYGEN CYCLE

Most of the oxygen in the air is produced by plants. Animals, including us, breathe that oxygen in. We use the oxygen to make the systems in our bodies work.

We breathe out carbon dioxide. Plants take in this carbon dioxide and use the carbon to create sugars—food. Plants then give off oxygen and the cycle begins again.

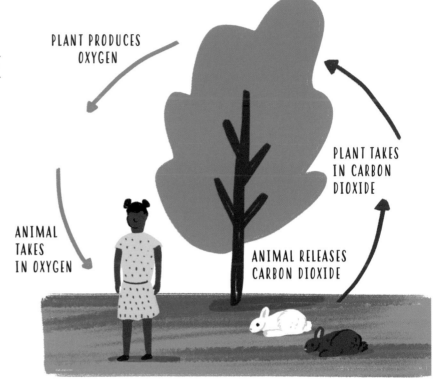

PLANT PRODUCES OXYGEN

PLANT TAKES IN CARBON DIOXIDE

ANIMAL TAKES IN OXYGEN

ANIMAL RELEASES CARBON DIOXIDE

O₂ TAKE A DEEP BREATH

All animal cells need oxygen for **respiration**. Every animal cell needs oxygen to function. Animals take in oxygen and it reacts with the glucose (sugar) from food to create energy.

Respiration is the process that takes in oxygen and exchanges it for carbon dioxide and water, which are waste products. Humans breathe and the oxygen needed for respiration is transported throughout our body in red blood cells.

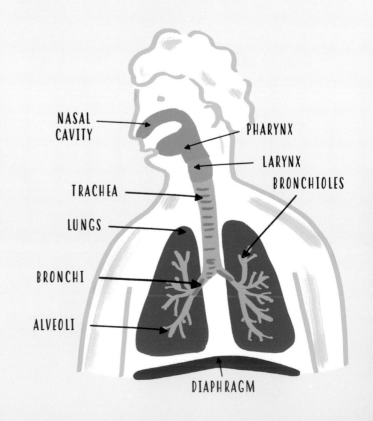

NASAL CAVITY

PHARYNX

LARYNX
BRONCHIOLES

TRACHEA

LUNGS

BRONCHI

ALVEOLI

DIAPHRAGM

Carl Wilhelm Scheele discovered oxygen in 1772. He called it "fire air" because it was needed for things to burn. Scientists call burning combustion. It is a chemical reaction. The reaction gives off heat, light, and other chemicals.

Fires start when combustible material (something that burns), together with oxygen, is heated. If it is above the "flash point" for the material, a fire starts. Flames are the part of fire that we can see.

Flames are made up of oxygen, water in gas form, and carbon dioxide. The shade of the flame depends on the material being burned and any impurities. We just see the flames as pretty reds, oranges, and yellows!

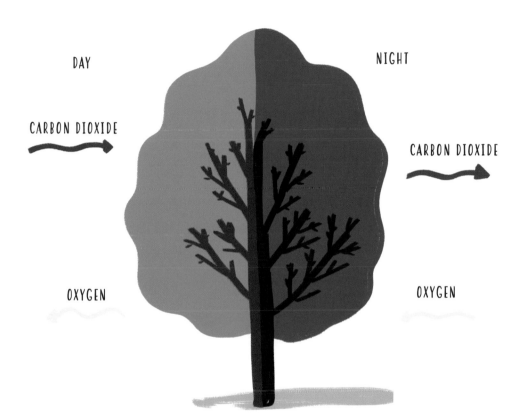

DAY

CARBON DIOXIDE

OXYGEN

NIGHT

CARBON DIOXIDE

OXYGEN

Plants also use respiration to create energy (for growth and reproduction) from the sugars they make during photosynthesis.

When it is dark, plants respire, but do not photosynthesize as this requires light. That means they take in oxygen and release carbon dioxide at night. During the day, in bright light, plants photosynthesize faster than they respire, so oxygen is released and carbon dioxide is taken in.

OUT OF CURIOSITY

Many animals that live in water can absorb oxygen that is dissolved in water using body parts called gills. Some water-living animals, such as seals and crocodiles, have lungs that take in oxygen from the air. They need to swim to the water surface to breathe.

CARBON DIOXIDE

Do you like fizzy drinks? Those sparkling bubbles that stream to the top of your glass, and make that yummy fizzy taste, are carbon dioxide!

CO_2

Carbon dioxide is about much more than soda, though. Its chemical **formula** is CO_2, which means that each molecule is made of one carbon and two oxygen atoms. This common chemical makes up around 0.041% of Earth's atmosphere.

 ## PHOTOSYNTHESIS

When trees and plants **photosynthesize** (use the energy from the sun to create food; see page 62) they remove CO_2 from the air. That is a good thing, because too much CO_2 building up in the atmosphere is bad for the planet.

CO_2 is a **greenhouse gas** (see pages 60–61), which means that too much can cause climate change. Plants and trees extract CO_2 from the air during the day, but animals and humans breathe it out.

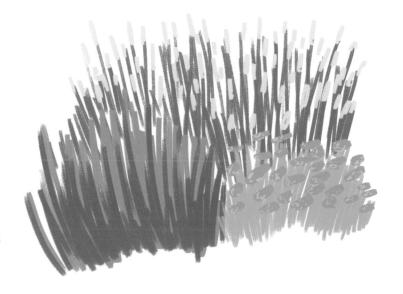

FRESH AIR

If you are in a room that feels stuffy and you are drowsy, it may be because there are lots of people in there breathing out CO_2. Carbon dioxide is a waste product of our body processes, so you need to open a window to get some "fresh" air!

OUT OF CURIOSITY

CO_2 has quite a high freezing point, so it can be frozen and stored as "dry ice" to use in stage shows! Dry ice can make fog when it is dropped into warm water. Carbon dioxide gas is released from the ice as a very cold gas. This makes the water in the air condense and form droplets which we see as "fog."

CARBON

Carbon is absolutely fundamental to life, because it is found in all organic compounds. Organic compounds make up cells and carry out life processes—such as when animals eat and digest food, or breathe.

CARBON CYCLE

When animals (including humans) eat, they take in carbon in the form of proteins and carbohydrates. Oxygen in the cells of animals combines with the food and produces energy. That allows animals to move and grow, for example. A waste product of this process is carbon. The carbon is combined with oxygen to form carbon dioxide, which animals release into the atmosphere as they exhale, or breathe out.

Carbon atoms are constantly moving through living things, in the atmosphere, in the oceans, in the soil, and in the Earth's crust. This is called the carbon cycle.

DIAMOND

This abundant **element** can take many different forms. It can be a super-hard substance used in cutting machinery and engagement rings. Diamond crystals can develop into several different shapes. The most common is the diamond shape. Diamond crystals can also form cubes. These are very strong structures— that's why diamonds are so strong!

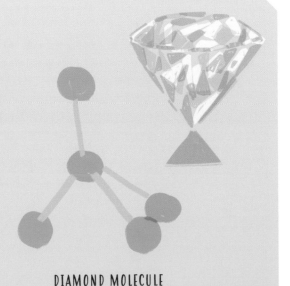

DIAMOND MOLECULE

GRAPHITE

Carbon can also be a slippery, electrical **conductor**—graphite. Graphite is used as a **lubricant** to make things move more easily (such as machine parts) and can also be used for drawing as, when it is rubbed on paper, some of the graphite is left on the page. Graphite has carbon atoms arranged in hexagons.

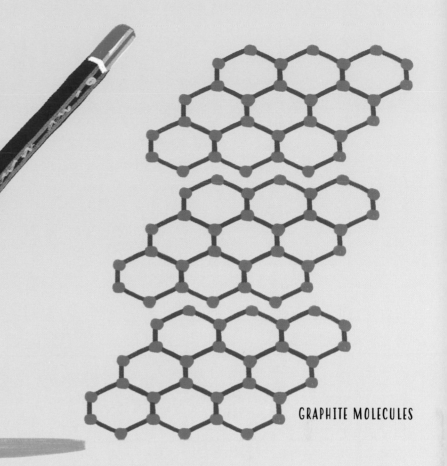

PENCIL LEAD IS MADE OF GRAPHITE

GRAPHITE MOLECULES

BUCKMINSTERFULLERENE

Another form of carbon is buckminsterfullerene, or C_{60}. These were the first **nanoparticles** ever discovered, back in 1985. They are made up of 60 carbon atoms and shaped like a hollow soccer ball.

Buckminsterfullerene is unique—the only molecule of a single element to create a hollow spherical "cage." Its atoms are arranged in a collection of 12 pentagons and 20 hexagons. Nicknamed 'buckyballs," these molecules are named after American inventor Buckminster Fuller, who designed many buildings based on geodesic domes, which are round structures that can withstand heavy loads.

C_{60} is very stable and this means scientists see a world of possibilities for this tiny "cage." Research is ongoing into using buckyballs for super-powerful batteries, cancer treatments, rocket fuel, and new types of plastics.

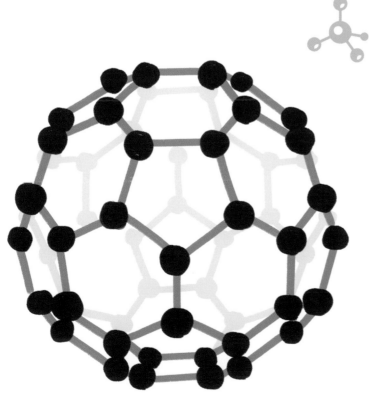

BUCKYBALL MOLECULE

NITROGEN

Do you think oxygen is the main element found in air?
If so—think again! Nitrogen (N) makes up an amazing 78%
of the air we breathe. It is a clear, smell-free, taste-free gas.

CHLOROPHYLL

Nitrogen was discovered in 1772 by Daniel Rutherford. It is vital to many processes in living things. It is found in **chlorophyll** in plants (see page 62), in protein, and in **DNA** in animals—including you.

Plants are hungry for nitrogen, and that is why it is sometimes applied to soil to make it more fertile—to feed and nourish those hungry plants.

There is a downside though. Man-made nitrogen compounds can pollute when they run off in rain into streams and rivers. Nitrogen can poison aquatic life, like fish.

FIZZY DRINKS

Although many fizzy drinks have bubbles of carbon dioxide, the bubbles in beer are often nitrogen—though there is frequently some carbon dioxide as well. Nitrogen makes smaller bubbles than carbon dioxide, and the nitrogen bubbles make the smooth, creamy head that some beers have.

COOL...

Nitrogen is used in some food packaging to push out oxygen and prevent the food from spoiling. Some microbes (tiny forms of life) that can spoil food need oxygen for respiration, and cannot use nitrogen, so food stays fresher. It is also used as a coolant, in computers, to stop them from overheating. Nitrogen treatment is even used to treat warts and verrucae by freezing them!

NITRO-POWER!

The nitrogen-containing compound nitrous oxide is a gas sometimes used in hospitals and dental clinics. It can reduce pain and relax people who are having procedures that might make them anxious. Nitrous oxide is sometimes known as "laughing gas" because it makes people giggly. This gas can also be used to increase the power of engines in racing cars—and then it gets called "nitrous."

BOOM!

Another nitrogen-based compound, nitroglycerin, is a liquid that can be used to create dynamite for the construction industry. It is a dangerous explosive that uses chemistry to create a big bang to demolish things, and prepare ground and rock for work.

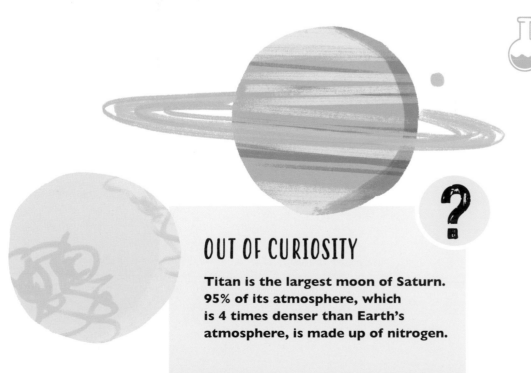

OUT OF CURIOSITY

Titan is the largest moon of Saturn. 95% of its atmosphere, which is 4 times denser than Earth's atmosphere, is made up of nitrogen.

OZONE

Have you ever smelled a tangy, electrical smell when there has been a lightning storm? That's ozone (O_3)—three bonded atoms of oxygen! Ozone is sometimes produced when a charge of electricity (in this case, lightning) passes through the air.

Ozone can be both a blessing and a curse. It is not found in living things, but plays a key role in protecting them. As a gas in Earth's upper atmosphere, it shields the planet from **ultraviolet** (UV) rays from the Sun. Without it, life on land would be damaged.

THE OZONE LAYER

A thin layer of ozone circles the Earth 10 to 50 km (6 to 31 miles) up. Humans cause problems by releasing chemicals that damage this precious ozone layer. The first of these to be identified was chlorofluorocarbons (or CFCs), which are used in aerosol sprays such as hair spray and deodorant. The production of CFCs is now banned around the world, but other chemicals, including nitrous oxide (see page 57) from car exhausts, still cause damage.

Chemicals that damage the ozone layer have made thin patches in it, usually called holes, which grow larger and smaller each year. The holes allow dangerous ultraviolet rays to travel through. They can cause cancer, eye diseases, and other health problems. The ozone layer seems to be healing itself and by 2170 might be fully repaired.

SMOG MAKER

When found lower down in the atmosphere, far below the natural ozone layer, ozone can be very polluting. Ozone is created in the lower atmosphere when gases from car exhausts mix with sunlight. Ozone can create smog (smoky fog) in cities and cause breathing difficulties. So we need ozone—but only in the right place!

GREENHOUSE GASES

Like ozone, greenhouse gases can both help and harm living things. These gases in our planet's atmosphere trap heat. They allow sunlight to pass through, but do not let all the heat back out of the atmosphere again, so the Earth stays warm. By absorbing **infrared radiation** and reflecting it back to Earth, they enable living things to survive.

If a planet has too many greenhouse gases in its atmosphere, it gets too hot. This means that water cannot remain in a liquid form. It evaporates. This happened to the planet Venus! Water is a vital ingredient in the process of photosynthesis, which is the basis for all life on Earth.

The main greenhouse gases are:

CARBON DIOXIDE   **METHANE**   **WATER VAPOR**

OZONE   **NITROUS OXIDE**

FOSSIL FUELS

The actions of human beings can increase the amount of greenhouse gases in the atmosphere. Burning fossil fuels such as coal, oil, and natural gas releases greenhouse gases. Chopping down forests (called deforestation) means there are fewer trees to absorb carbon dioxide—and it releases the carbon stored by the trees.

This leads to climate change as the Earth gets hotter. Global heating causes habitats to change, and animals and plants cannot adapt quickly enough to keep up. They may go hungry and even become extinct as a result.

Climate change also causes extreme weather patterns, such as typhoons and hurricanes. Sea levels rise as the polar ice caps melt, and flooding occurs.

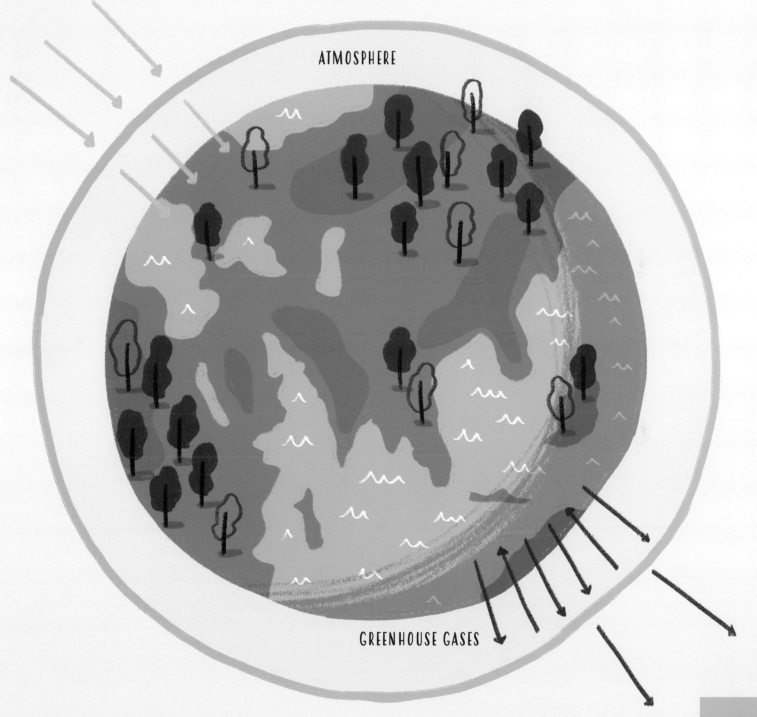

Sunlight passes through the greenhouse gases and warms the Earth

OUTER SPACE

ATMOSPHERE

GREENHOUSE GASES

The Earth warms up and gives out heat. Some heat passes back out through the greenhouse gases, but some is trapped inside, keeping the Earth warm.

CHLOROPHYLL

Chlorophyll is like green magic! This organic compound is found in **chloroplasts**—the tiny "factories" inside leaves. Chloroplasts use water, carbon dioxide, and energy from sunlight to produce food for the plant in the form of glucose, a type of sugar. Chlorophyll is the key to this process, which we call **photosynthesis**. It also make leaves green!

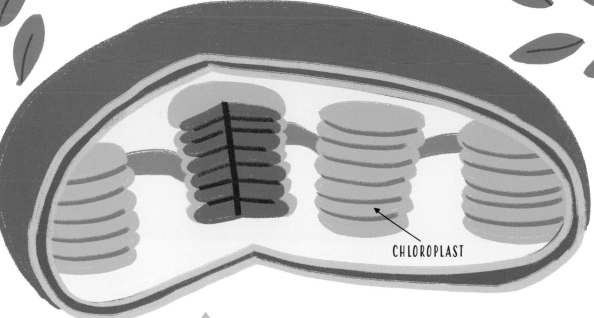

CHLOROPLAST

CHLOROPHYLL

Chlorophylls are special **pigments** found inside chloroplasts. Chlorophyll is the material that absorbs light and turns it into chemical energy, via photosynthesis. Chemical energy is stored in the bonds of chemical compounds, such as between atoms and molecules. The energy is released when chemical reactions happen. Without this process, plants could not live. Plants are at the bottom of most food chains, so without chlorophyll it would be hard for many living things to find food.

FOOD CHAIN

PLANT

INSECT

AUTUMN SHADES

We see chlorophyll as green, because it doesn't absorb the green wavelengths of light. Those are reflected from plants, so they appear green. The three pigments that shade leaves are chlorophyll, anthocyanins (that cause red leaves), and carotenes (which cause yellow leaves). As the temperature falls before winter, chlorophyll breaks down in deciduous trees (the ones that lose their leaves later in the year), so the leaves change their shade as the green fades. That's why we see trees in blazing oranges, reds, and yellows!

MOUSE

OWL

The chemical energy stored in photosynthesis travels up the food chain, as animals eat plants and other animals.

PROTEIN

Proteins make up all of the major structural tissue (such as muscle tissue) in animals—and that includes you! Proteins are long **polymers**—molecules shaped like a chain. Our bodies can produce 13 types of amino acid (the building blocks that make up protein), but there are nine we need and cannot make.

We obtain these essential amino acids by eating food that is rich in protein. Complete protein contains all of the amino acids we need. It is found in dairy products, eggs, soy, meat, and fish.

Incomplete protein sources include nuts, grains, some vegetables, and fruit. Vegetarians combine foods carefully to make sure their bodies take in all of the amino acids they need for their bodies to grow and repair. Eggs are considered to contain the highest-quality, most usable protein of all foods. The proteins in some foods, such as gluten in wheat, can cause allergic reactions in some people.

PROTEIN IN OUR BODIES

Fibrous protein molecules are long chains that group together into bundles and are differently arranged to make muscle, fingernails—and even hair. The protein that makes up hair, nails, and outer layers of skin is called keratin. After water, protein is the most common type of substance found in the human body.

SKIN CELLS

SUPER USEFUL

Proteins help to regulate and maintain life processes, speeding up **chemical reactions** in your cells. The instructions for making proteins are coded into your **genes**. An example of a protein found in your body is hemoglobin. This protein is found in red blood cells and it contains iron. It transports oxygen around your body.

OUT OF CURIOSITY

Insects contain high levels of protein, and are a nutritious food source. Some insects contain more protein than meat or fish!

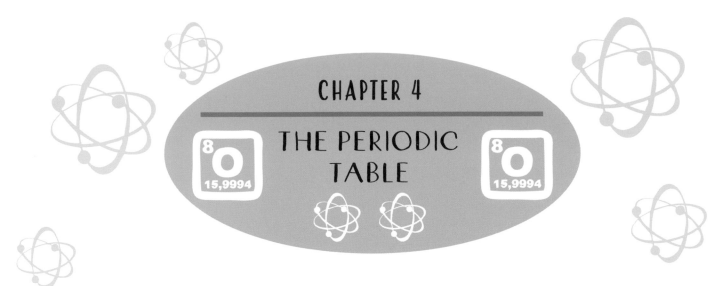

CHAPTER 4

THE PERIODIC TABLE

The periodic table is a table that arranges the known elements in a list in order of their atomic number. It was invented by the Russian chemist Dmitry Ivanovich Mendeleyev in 1869.

The first periodic table did not look the same as the version we use now: it was revised several times as scientists discovered more about different elements and their properties. The version scientists use today has been the same since the mid-1900s.

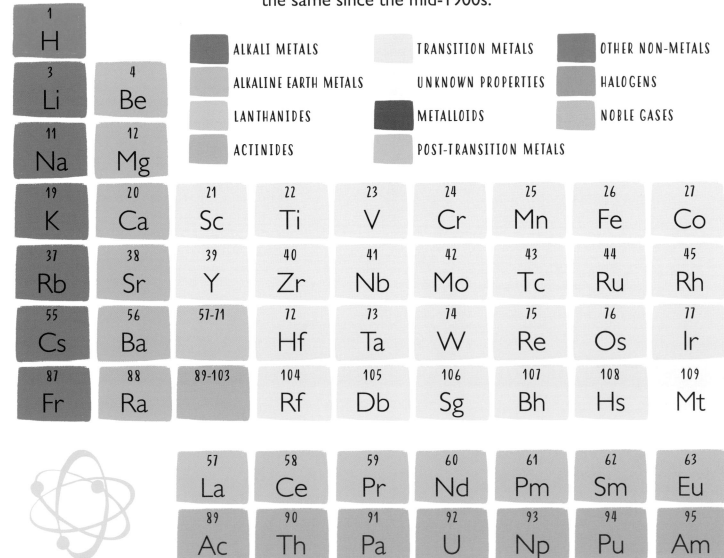

ATOMIC NUMBER

The atomic number of an element is the same as the number of protons in the atom of the element. The periodic table starts with the lowest atomic number and moves through the elements to the highest number. The table is used by chemists to observe patterns and relationships between elements.

The table is arranged into periods, which are the rows across the table. Each period has a number from 1 to 7. Every element in the first period (the top row) has one **orbital** for its electrons. All of the elements in the second period have 2 orbitals and so on.

GROUPS

Columns of elements are called groups. These groups are numbered 1 to 18.

Elements arranged in groups have electrons arranged in similar ways. This means they behave in similar ways, and have similar chemical properties. That helps chemists to predict how elements might react in a given situation.

For example, magnesium (Mg) and calcium (Ca) are both in column 2 and share similarities.

OUT OF CURIOSITY

Francium is the world's rarest naturally occurring element—only a few grams are on Earth at any one time!

							2 He
		5 B	6 C	7 N	8 O	9 F	10 Ne
		13 Al	14 Si	15 P	16 S	17 Cl	18 Ar
28 Ni	29 Cu	30 Zn	31 Ga	32 Ge	33 As	34 Se	35 Br	36 Kr
46 Pd	47 Ag	48 Cd	49 In	50 Sn	51 Sb	52 Te	53 I	54 Xe
78 Pt	79 Au	80 Hg	81 Tl	82 Pb	83 Bi	84 Po	85 At	86 Rn
110 Ds	111 Rg	112 Cn	113 Nh	114 Fl	115 Mc	116 Lv	117 Ts	118 Og

64 Gd	65 Tb	66 Dy	67 Ho	68 Er	69 Tm	70 Yb	71 Lu
96 Cm	97 Bk	98 Cf	99 Es	100 Fm	101 Md	102 No	103 Lr

NON-METALS

Non-metals are elements that are usually solid or gas under standard conditions. They are found in the top right-hand corner of the periodic table, except hydrogen. They have similar chemical properties that are different to elements that are metals:

NON-METALS

1 H																	2 He
3 Li	4 Be											5 B	6 C	7 N	8 O	9 F	10 Ne
11 Na	12 Mg											13 Al	14 Si	15 P	16 S	17 Cl	18 Ar
19 K	20 Ca	21 Sc	22 Ti	23 V	24 Cr	25 Mn	26 Fe	27 Co	28 Ni	29 Cu	30 Zn	31 Ga	32 Ge	33 As	34 Se	35 Br	36 Kr
37 Rb	38 Sr	39 Y	40 Zr	41 Nb	42 Mo	43 Tc	44 Ru	45 Rh	46 Pd	47 Ag	48 Cd	49 In	50 Sn	51 Sb	52 Te	53 I	54 Xe
55 Cs	56 Ba	57-71	72 Hf	73 Ta	74 W	75 Re	76 Os	77 Ir	78 Pt	79 Au	80 Hg	81 Tl	82 Pb	83 Bi	84 Po	85 At	86 Rn
87 Fr	88 Ra	89-103	104 Rf	105 Db	106 Sg	107 Bh	108 Hs	109 Mt	110 Ds	111 Rg	112 Cn	113 Nh	114 Fl	115 Mc	116 Lv	117 Ts	118 Og

57 La	58 Ce	59 Pr	60 Nd	61 Pm	62 Sm	63 Eu	64 Gd	65 Tb	66 Dy	67 Ho	68 Er	69 Tm	70 Yb	71 Lu
89 Ac	90 Th	91 Pa	92 U	93 Np	94 Pu	95 Am	96 Cm	97 Bk	98 Cf	99 Es	100 Fm	101 Md	102 No	103 Lr

- DULL, NOT SHINY
- POOR CONDUCTOR OF ELECTRICITY
- NOT DUCTILE (STRETCHABLE)
- BRITTLE, NOT EASILY BENT IN A SOLID STATE
- GOOD INSULATORS AGAINST COLD AND HEAT
- GAIN ELECTRONS DURING REACTIONS

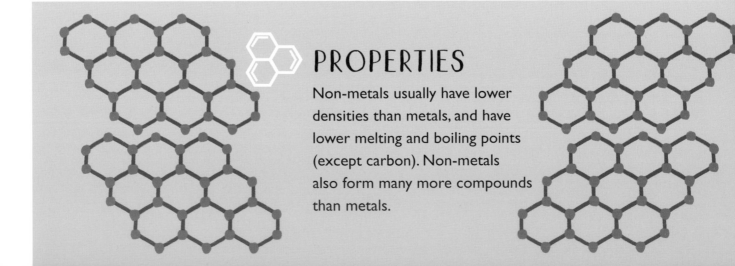

PROPERTIES

Non-metals usually have lower densities than metals, and have lower melting and boiling points (except carbon). Non-metals also form many more compounds than metals.

LIVING THINGS

Living things are made up almost entirely of non-metals. The human body is around 65% oxygen, 18% carbon, 10% hydrogen, and 3% nitrogen.

TABLE OF NON-METALS

NUMBER	SYMBOL	ELEMENT
1	H	Hydrogen
2	He	Helium
6	C	Carbon
7	N	Nitrogen
8	O	Oxygen
9	F	Fluorine
10	Ne	Neon
15	P	Phosphorus
16	S	Sulfur
17	Cl	Chlorine
18	Ar	Argon
34	Se	Selenium
35	Br	Bromine
36	Kr	Krypton
53	I	Iodine
54	Xe	Xenon
85	At	Astatine
86	Rn	Radon
117	Ts	Tennessine
118	Og	Oganesson

OUT OF CURIOSITY

Two of the non-metal gases, hydrogen and helium, make up 99% of normal matter in the Universe. Nitrogen at 78% and oxygen at 21% make up most of Earth's atmosphere. Our water is made from the non-metals hydrogen and oxygen.

HALOGENS

Halogens are the elements in group 17 of the periodic table. Halogen means "salt-becomer," because the Greek word "*hals*" means "salt," and "gen" means "to make."

Halogens are very reactive, with fluorine being one of the most reactive elements in existence. The reactivity of the halogens decreases as you move down the column in the periodic table.

HALOGENS

1 H																	2 He
3 Li	4 Be											5 B	6 C	7 N	8 O	9 F	10 Ne
11 Na	12 Mg											13 Al	14 Si	15 P	16 S	17 Cl	18 Ar
19 K	20 Ca	21 Sc	22 Ti	23 V	24 Cr	25 Mn	26 Fe	27 Co	28 Ni	29 Cu	30 Zn	31 Ga	32 Ge	33 As	34 Se	35 Br	36 Kr
37 Rb	38 Sr	39 Y	40 Zr	41 Nb	42 Mo	43 Tc	44 Ru	45 Rh	46 Pd	47 Ag	48 Cd	49 In	50 Sn	51 Sb	52 Te	53 I	54 Xe
55 Cs	56 Ba	57-71	72 Hf	73 Ta	74 W	75 Re	76 Os	77 Ir	78 Pt	79 Au	80 Hg	81 Tl	82 Pb	83 Bi	84 Po	85 At	86 Rn
87 Fr	88 Ra	89-103	104 Rf	105 Db	106 Sg	107 Bh	108 Hs	109 Mt	110 Ds	111 Rg	112 Cn	113 Nh	114 Fl	115 Mc	116 Lv	117 Ts	118 Og

		57 La	58 Ce	59 Pr	60 Nd	61 Pm	62 Sm	63 Eu	64 Gd	65 Tb	66 Dy	67 Ho	68 Er	69 Tm	70 Yb	71 Lu
		89 Ac	90 Th	91 Pa	92 U	93 Np	94 Pu	95 Am	96 Cm	97 Bk	98 Cf	99 Es	100 Fm	101 Md	102 No	103 Lr

DANGER!

The elements in this group are fluorine (F), chlorine (Cl), bromine (Br), iodine (I), and astatine (At). Halogens are all quite toxic. Fluorine gas is lethal. Breathing air that contains a tiny 0.1% concentration of fluorine can kill you!

COMPOUNDS

Halogens form acids when combined with hydrogen (H). Compounds containing halogens are called halides. Halogens have low melting points and low boiling points.

WHERE IN THE WORLD?

All halogens are found in compounds in the Earth's crust. Fluorine and chlorine are abundant, but iodine and bromine are quite rare. Astatine, on the other hand, is one of the rarest naturally occurring elements on Earth.

USES FOR HALOGENS

Halogen light bulbs and lamps have a tungsten filament in a quartz container. The gas around the filament is a halogen.

Halogen lamps glow with a whiter light than other bulbs, and get up to a higher temperature. The bulbs need to be made from fused quartz to reduce breakage.

Chlorine and bromine are both used as disinfectants, to sterilize things and to kill bacteria, even in wounds and drinking water. That smell in swimming pools is chlorine.

Sodium hypochlorite is produced from chlorine, and is the main ingredient of bleach. It is used for cleaning, laundry, and for bleaching paper and fabric. It burns the skin and eyes, so never touch it.

Fluoride is added to water and toothpaste in tiny quantities to fight tooth decay.

OUT OF CURIOSITY

Bromine smells bad. It gets its name from the Greek word "*bromos*," which means stench!

NOBLE GASES

Noble gases are in group 18 of the periodic table. They do not react with other elements. They have no smell and they are clear. As you move down the periodic table, the elements become rarer.

There are six noble gases:

HELIUM (He)   **NEON** (Ne)   **ARGON** (Ar)

KRYPTON (Kr)   **XENON** (Xe)   **RADON** (Rn)

WILLIAM RAMSAY

Many of the noble gases were discovered (or isolated) by Sir William Ramsay. He received the Nobel Prize for Chemistry in 1904 for the discovery of "inert gaseous elements in air."

OUT OF CURIOSITY

Helium has the lowest melting point (-272°C, or -458 °F), and boiling point (-268.9°C, or -452.1 °F) of any substance.

USES FOR NOBLE GASES

Noble gases have very low boiling points. That makes them useful as refrigerants, to keep things cool. Helium in a liquid form is used by hospitals in MRI (Magnetic Resonance Imaging) machines. MRI scanners use strong magnets (which the helium keeps cool) and a type of radio wave to examine organs and structures in the human body.

Helium is also added to the breathing mix used by divers on deep dives. Gases such as nitrogen and oxygen are absorbed by your blood and your body tissues, but helium is not highly soluble in liquids. Adding it to tanks used by divers makes **oxygen toxicity**, which is lung damage caused by breathing too much oxygen.

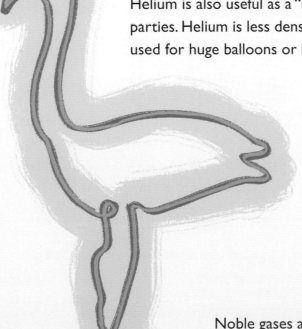

Helium is also useful as a "lifting gas"— you may have seen helium balloons floating at parties. Helium is less dense than air, so things filled with helium rise. Helium is also used for huge balloons or blimps, as it is very light and does not burn, so it is safe.

Noble gases are often used in lighting because they are not very reactive. Noble gases glow brightly, in different shades—and they are found in "neon" lights.

Noble gases are used in medicine, for example in lasers used by surgeons. Helium is effective as an asthma treatment. Xenon puts people to sleep for operations. Radon is used in radiotherapy.

Noble gases are very helpful to chemists. They are used in laboratories to stabilize reactions that would normally happen too quickly.

Argon is used in welding. It is denser than air, so it stops air from getting to the metal being welded. It is inert (does not react), so the hot metal does not oxidize. That would spoil the welded piece.

ALKALI METALS

Alkali metals are in group 1 of the periodic table, although hydrogen isn't one of them. Pure forms of the alkali metals are silver in shade and soft—you could cut them easily with a knife.

They react really strongly with water—some explosively—and have to be stored carefully. They are mostly stored under a layer of oil to stop them from **reacting**. In the air, they react to the oxygen (oxidize) and turn black. They are **malleable** and **ductile**, and good conductors of both heat and electricity.

POTASSIUM

The alkali metals are:

LITHIUM (Li)	**SODIUM** (Na)
POTASSIUM (K)	**CESIUM** (Cs)
FRANCIUM (Fr)	**RUBIDIUM** (Rb)

UNSTABLE

Alkali metals are never found in nature in their pure forms, as they are so unstable that they react quickly and combine to make other substances.

Sodium is in sodium chloride (NaCl) or table salt—the type used in cooking! It is also in sodium hydroxide (NaOH), commonly called caustic soda. This is used in cleaning and is a very strong and corrosive base.

ATOMIC CLOCKS

Caesium and rubidium are used to make atomic clocks. Caesium clocks are said to be the most accurate clocks, keeping the best time.

Potassium is used in the manufacture of fertilizers.

FERTILIZER

 # FLAME FACTS:

Alkali metals burn with a variety of tinted flames.

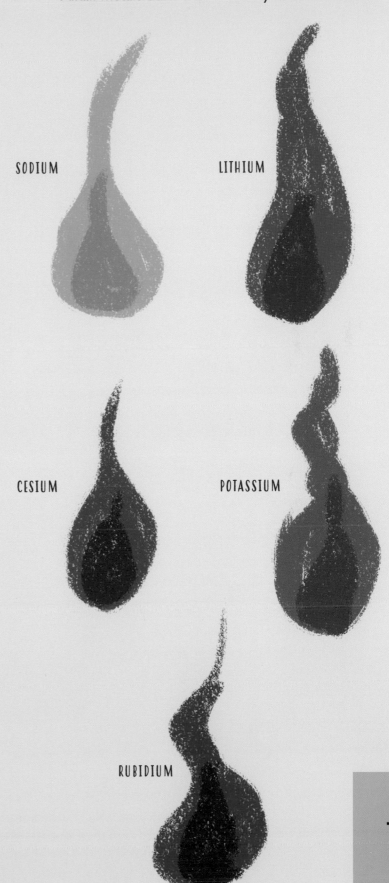

SODIUM

LITHIUM

CESIUM

POTASSIUM

RUBIDIUM

ALKALINE EARTH METALS

Alkaline earth metals are the second group on the periodic table.
They are related to, but not as reactive as, the alkali metals.
They are mainly silver in shade and soft, and react with halogens
to form salts—compounds called halides. They occur in nature,
but only as compounds and **minerals**.

The alkaline earth
metals are:

BERYLLIUM (Be)

MAGNESIUM (Mg)

CALCIUM (Ca)

STRONTIUM (Sr)

BARIUM (Ba)

RADIUM (Ra)

Many of the alkaline earth
metals were discovered
by Sir Humphry Davy (the
man who invented the Davy
safety lamp for miners)
including calcium, barium,
strontium, and magnesium.

OUT OF CURIOSITY

**Radium is formed by the radioactive decay of uranium and is dangerous to
handle. It is scary to think that it used to be an ingredient in glow-in-the-dark
paints which were used for many items around the house.**

**It was discovered by Marie and Pierre Curie. It has been used in medicine,
creating radon gas from radium chloride to be used in cancer treatments such
as radiotherapy.**

pH

Alkaline earth metals form solutions with a pH greater than 7. This makes them bases, or "alkaline."

Calcium and magnesium are important to living things. For example, magnesium is found in chlorophyll in green plants.

HUMAN BODIES AND ALKALINE METALS

Humans and many animals use calcium to build strong bones and teeth. Magnesium helps to regulate your body temperature.

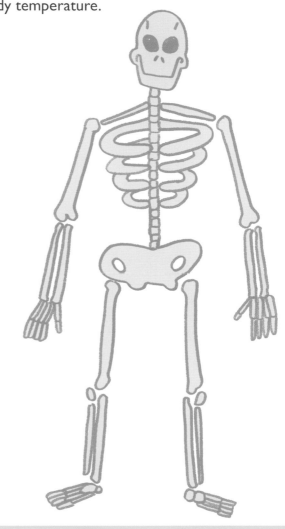

FLAME FACTS:

Alkaline earth metals burn with tinted flames.

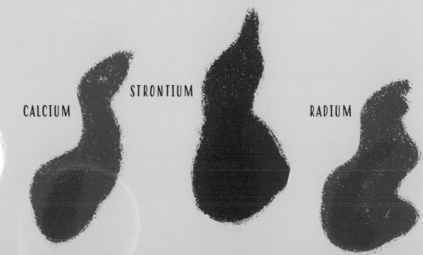

BERYLLIUM

MAGNESIUM

CALCIUM

STRONTIUM

RADIUM

TRANSITION METALS

Transition metals are found in the middle of the periodic table.
It is called the "d block." There are 35 elements in this section.
They all have similar properties.

They are harder than alkaline earth metals and less reactive.
They make up the largest section of the periodic table, from columns
3 to 12, although sometimes the elements in column 12 are not included as
part of the transition metal group (zinc (Zn), cadmium (Cd), mercury (Hg),
and copernicium (Cn)). Most metals are transition metals.

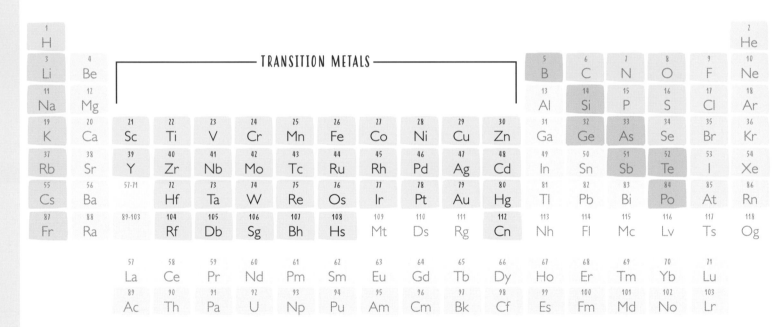

⚙ COMMON PROPERTIES

Transition metals can form many compounds.
They conduct electricity and have high
melting and boiling points. They have higher
densities than the alkaline earth metals.

When they are freshly cut, transition metals
are shiny. They are strong and hard.

PRECIOUS METALS

"Precious" metals, such as the types we wear as necklaces and rings, are transition metals: silver, gold, copper, platinum, and titanium.

REACTIONS

Transition metals react slowly with oxygen at room temperature, but some (like copper) react with oxygen when they are heated. Copper (Cu) + oxygen (O) = copper oxide (CuO).

Transition metals react slowly with cold water, or not at all. Iron (Fe) reacts with water (H_2O) and oxygen (O) to make rust, or iron oxide (Fe_2O_3)

HEALTHY BODIES

Some transition metals are needed by the human body to keep it healthy. We need iron to make blood, and zinc and chromium for other key processes in our bodies.

METALLOIDS

A metalloid is a strange element that has the properties of both metal and non-metal elements. For example, it might be brittle like a non-metal, but shiny like a metal. It could be a conductor of electricity like a metal, but dull like a non-metal.

Metalloids can form alloys with metals. Some are semi-conductors, like silicon and germanium. That means they only conduct electricity under special conditions.

WHERE IN THE WORLD?

The most abundant (found most often) metalloid on Earth is silicon (Si), and the rarest is tellurium (Te).

Other metalloids are boron (B), germanium (Ge), arsenic (As), and antimony (Sb). Selenium (Se) and polonium (Po) are sometimes included in this group as well.

Unlike other families of elements, metalloids are arranged in a diagonal line on the periodic table.

METALLOIDS

1 H																	2 He
3 Li	4 Be											5 B	6 C	7 N	8 O	9 F	10 Ne
11 Na	12 Mg											13 Al	14 Si	15 P	16 S	17 Cl	18 Ar
19 K	20 Ca	71 Sc	22 Ti	23 V	24 Cr	25 Mn	26 Fe	27 Co	28 Ni	29 Cu	30 Zn	31 Ga	32 Ge	33 As	34 Se	35 Br	36 Kr
37 Rb	38 Sr	39 Y	40 Zr	41 Nb	42 Mo	43 Tc	44 Ru	45 Rh	46 Pd	47 Ag	48 Cd	49 In	50 Sn	51 Sb	52 Te	53 I	54 Xe
55 Cs	56 Ba	57-71	72 Hf	73 Ta	74 W	75 Re	76 Os	77 Ir	78 Pt	79 Au	80 Hg	81 Tl	82 Pb	83 Bi	84 Po	85 At	86 Rn
87 Fr	88 Ra	89-103	104 Rf	105 Db	106 Sg	107 Bh	108 Hs	109 Mt	110 Ds	111 Rg	112 Cn	113 Nh	114 Fl	115 Mc	116 Lv	117 Ts	118 Og

	57 La	58 Ce	59 Pr	60 Nd	61 Pm	62 Sm	63 Eu	64 Gd	65 Tb	66 Dy	67 Ho	68 Er	69 Tm	70 Yb	71 Lu
	89 Ac	90 Th	91 Pa	92 U	93 Np	94 Pu	95 Am	96 Cm	97 Bk	98 Cf	99 Es	100 Fm	101 Md	102 No	103 Lr

SILICON

Silicon is a common metalloid. It is a **semiconductor**, which makes it incredibly useful for technology.

Silicon is one of the most important materials in the manufacture of electronics such as mobile phones and computers. You will have technology containing silicon in your house right now!

SILICON VALLEY

This is an area near San Francisco where many computer-related companies are based. The silicon wafers used in computers are made by melting sand (silica). These are polished and then made to hold thousands of tiny transistors, which can amplify or switch electronic signals. Tiny triangles of these wafers are then cut and fitted into central processing units (CPUs), just like the one in your computer.

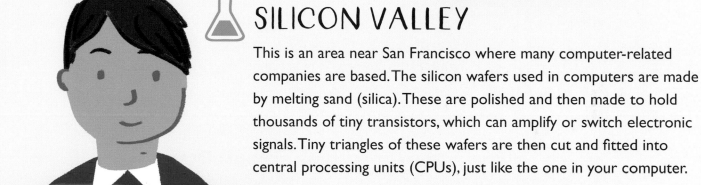

DANGER!

Arsenic is a highly poisonous metalloid. In fact, it is one of the most poisonous elements that exists! Arsenic is used to harden alloys, especially copper and lead alloys. It is also used as an ingredient in some wood preservatives, pesticides, and types of glass.

Antimony is used today in making metal alloys, but was used in cosmetics 5,000 years ago by the ancient Egyptians.

ACTINIDES AND LANTHANIDES

When you look at the periodic table, you see two rows at the bottom. These are sometimes called the "f block" of the periodic table.

One of the rows is called the lanthanides and the other is called the actinides. Some people call them rare-earth metals, and others call them inner-transition elements. There are 15 actinides—which are shown in purple at the bottom of page 83—and 15 lanthanides—shown in blue.

 ## WHERE IN THE WORLD?

Actinides and lanthanides are highly reactive with halogens. Lanthanides are naturally occurring on Earth. Some of the actinides are not naturally occurring and are only made in laboratories.

Lanthanides are metals that slowly turn into their hydroxides (react and combine with hydrogen molecules) when they are placed in water. They form a coating of oxide when exposed to air, like most metals.

 ## USES FOR ACTINIDES AND LANTHANIDES

Hybrid cars use lanthanides such as lanthanum, terbium, neodymium, and dysprosium in their batteries.

Americium (Am) is a synthetic radioactive element. It is an actinide, and is used in making smoke detectors.

URANIUM

Uranium (U), used in nuclear reactors to provide power, was once used to make glass—until it was found to be radioactive!

PLUTONIUM

Plutonium (Pu) was used to create the bomb that destroyed Nagasaki at the end of World War II. The bomb harnessed the awful power of a nuclear chain.

OUT OF CURIOSITY

The name actinium comes from the Greek word "*aktis*," which means beam or ray.

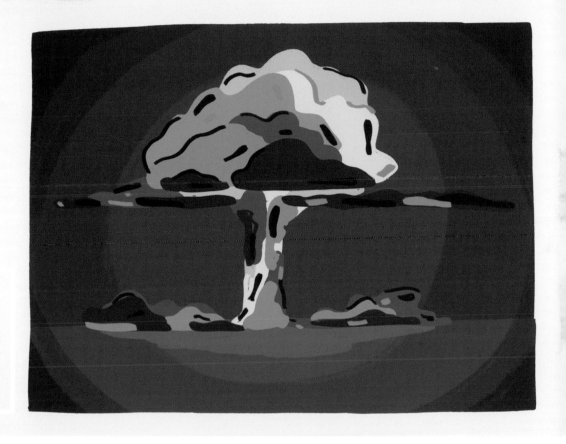

IT'S ALL IN THE NAME...

All of the elements in the actinide series are radioactive. Take a look at the list of names below—can you read them out loud? Some sound like names from science fiction, rather than science "fact"!

ACTINIUM (Ac)	THORIUM (Th)	PROTACTINIUM (Pa)	URANIUM (U)	NEPTUNIUM (Np)
PLUTONIUM (Pu)	AMERICIUM (Am)	CURIUM (Cm)	BERKELIUM (Bk)	CALIFORNIUM (Cf)
EINSTEINIUM (Es)	FERMIUM (Fm)	MENDELEVIUM (Md)	NOBELIUM (No)	LAWRENCIUM (Lr)
LANTHANUM (La)	CERIUM (Ce)	PRASEODYMIUM (Pr)	NEODYMIUM (Nd)	PROMETHIUM (Pm)
SAMARIUM (Sm)	EUROPIUM (Eu)	GADOLINIUM (Gd)	TERBIUM (Tb)	DYSPROSIUM (Dy)
HOLMIUM (Ho)	ERBIUM (Er)	THULIUM (Tm)	YTTERBIUM (Yb)	LUTETIUM (Lu)

POST-TRANSITION METALS

Post-transition metals, or "poor metals," are to the right of transition metals and to the left of metalloids on the periodic table.

There are discussions about which elements to include, but typically they include metals from groups 13, 14, and 15. They tend to be softer than other metals and have lower melting points. Post-transition metals are ductile and malleable, and conduct heat and electricity.

Included in this group are:

ALUMINUM (Al)   GALLIUM (Ga)   INDIUM (In)   TIN (Sn)

THALLIUM (Tl)   LEAD (Pb)   BISMUTH (Bi)

DECISIONS, DECISIONS...

Nihonium (Nh), flerovium (Fl), moscovium (Mo), and livermorium (Lv) are sometimes classified as post-transition metals—but not always. It's quite confusing!

ALUMINUM

The most common naturally occurring post-transition metal on Earth is aluminum. It is the third most abundant element in the Earth's crust.

Aluminum is light and relatively strong, so it is used to make containers, such as cans for carbonated (fizzy) drinks.

Aluminum was first identified as an element in 1825 and it was at first so expensive to produce that it was more highly valued than gold! Napoleon III was fascinated by it and funded experiments for using the element in the military.

HEALTH

Bismuth is used to make remedies for indigestion and heartburn. One dose contains around 262 milligrams of bismuth subsalicylate.

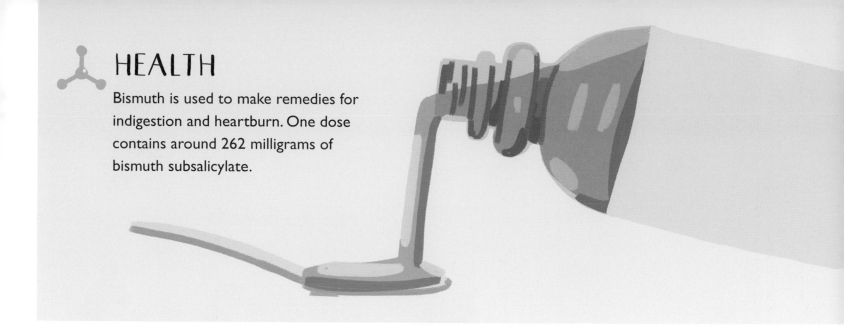

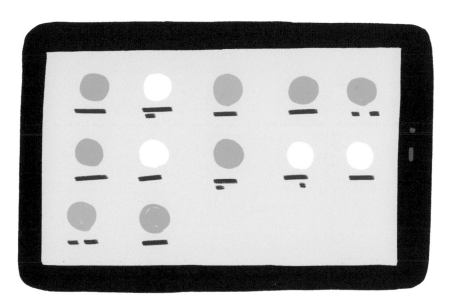

INDIUM

Indium is used to make electronics such as flat screens and touchscreens.

LEAD

In the past, lead was used to make toys because it could be melted and poured into molds easily and cheaply. Lead was also added to paint, but then it was found to cause poisoning.

Today, lead is still used in some products such as car batteries, but people understand that it can cause health problems if it is in regular contact with skin.

CHAPTER 5

IN THE LAB

Chemists are hard at work in laboratories every day. They are creating and watching reactions, developing new materials for industry, inventing new medicines, and more.

Chemists work in labs for a variety of reasons. Labs are safe, controlled environments to work with chemicals that might be dangerous if you just used them at home. They are sterile, which means germ-free. Conditions such as temperature can be easily controlled. The way labs are set up means it is easier for chemists to observe their experiments. "Variables"—things that could be changeable and affect the outcome of an experiment—can be controlled, and conditions can be kept stable.

Labs also have all of the equipment that chemists need. This equipment, such as powerful electron telescopes, is expensive and could be damaged if it was moved from place to place. All of the smaller tools and equipment they use, such as glass flasks, test tubes—and of course, chemicals!—are stored safely.

Chemists also work in teams. Working together in a lab means that observations of experiments can be shared and stored, and chemists can meet and collaborate (work together).

BUNSEN BURNER

Have you ever used a Bunsen burner? School students have been using them in science classes for decades. Using a Bunsen burner can be exciting, as long as you are careful and take safety precautions—it's still a flame, even if it is a controlled one!

DR. ROBERT BUNSEN

Bunsen burners produce flames that can be used for heating and sterilizing materials.

The Bunsen burner was invented by Dr. Robert Bunsen in 1855—although some historians believe he developed an earlier idea. Even if this is the case, it was Robert Bunsen who created the Bunsen burner as we know it—so it bears his name.

FASCINATING FLAMES

Chemists—and before them, alchemists—had been aware that sprinkling materials on flames could help to identify them by the shade the flame burned.

Potassium, for example, burns with a pale purple flame. This science knowledge is still used today in the creation of fireworks.

Bunsen saw a problem, however. He saw that the shade of flame itself could interfere with the identification of materials. If the substance created an orange or yellow flame, how would a chemist know when a flame is already naturally that shade?

FLAME TESTS

Bunsen created a burner that mixed methane gas and air in a constant stream, which could burn with a nearly clear flame. That made "flame tests" reliable. He published the design in 1857, but did not **patent** it. He did not want to get rich from his invention; he just enjoyed knowing that he had created something wonderful—and it is still used today!

OUT OF CURIOSITY

Robert Bunsen also invented the zinc-carbon battery, flash photography, and with his colleague Gustav Kirchhoff, he developed the scientific method of spectroscopy. They used spectroscopy to discover the elements rubidium and cesium.

GAS FLOW

Bunsen burners run on methane, which is mixed with air to create a flame that comes out of the top of the barrel. The flow of gas can be changed by using the valve.

Chemists use Bunsen burners in labs today to heat chemicals, or to create or speed a chemical reaction.

HOW DO BUNSEN BURNERS WORK?

Bunsen burners are made of metal, and have:

A) a barrel
B) a collar
C) air holes
D) a gas supply
E) a valve
F) a stand

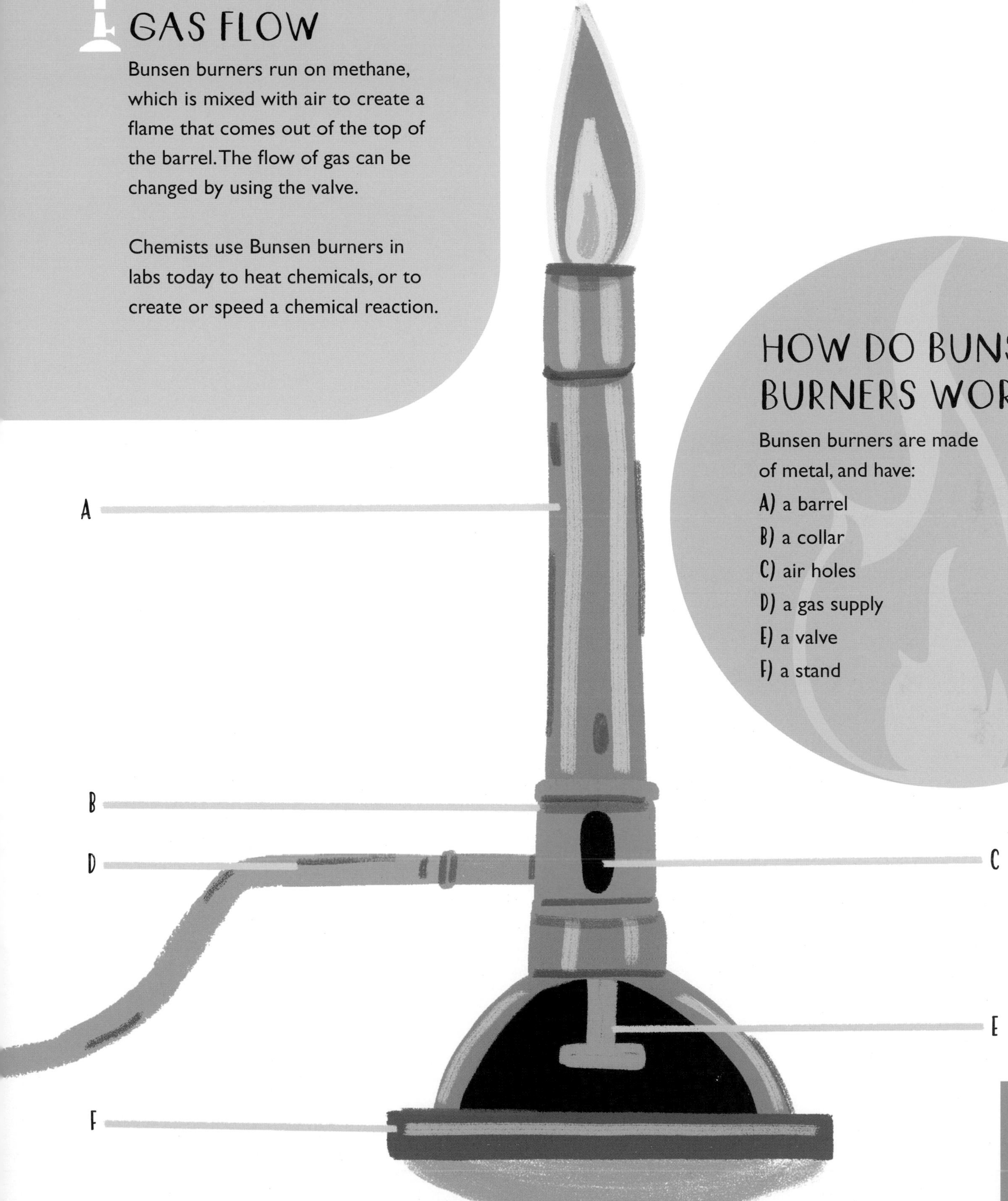

A

B

D

C

E

F

THERMOMETER

Thermometers measure temperature.
You may have used a medical thermometer
when you were sick, to check if you had a fever.

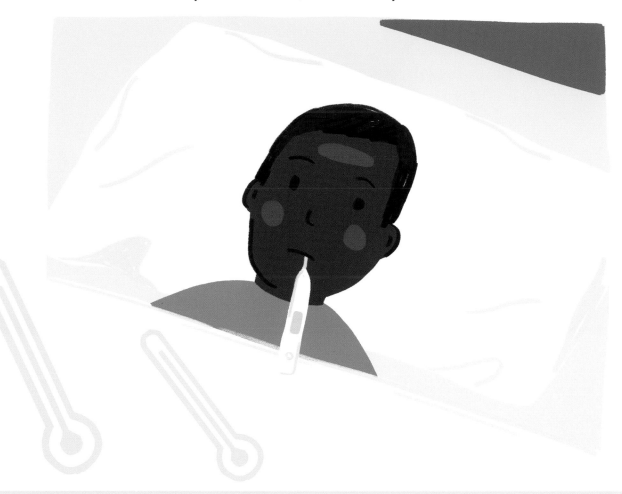

 ## MEDICAL THERMOMETERS

Thermometers contain materials that change as
they are heated and cooled. Liquid thermometers
contain liquids that expand and contract as the
temperature changes. This makes the liquid move
up and down the column.

Modern medical thermometers are often digital,
which gives an accurate reading. There is less room
for "operator error" as the temperature is read.

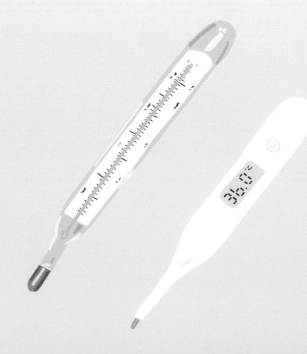

SCALES

Thermometers are marked in Fahrenheit and Celsius scales. These are standard measurements that mean the same thing wherever scientists are in the world.

The first thermometers to be invented were called thermoscopes. The Italian inventor Santorio was the first person to put a number scale on his air thermometer in 1612, so readings could be made.

FAHRENHEIT AND CELSIUS

In 1709, Gabriel Fahrenheit invented the first alcohol thermometer, and in 1714, the first mercury thermometer. In 1724 he introduced the scale that still bears his name.

In 1742, Anders Celsius introduced his centigrade or Celsius scale of temperature. This scale has 100 degrees between the freezing point 0°C and boiling point 100°C of pure water at sea level air pressure. It would not be until 1867 that Thomas Allbutt invented the first medical thermometer to take the temperature of patients.

LAB THERMOMETERS

In labs, thermometers are immersed in the substance being measured. They have long glass stems and a bulb at the bottom, filled with tinted liquid. You would not use them to measure the temperature of a patient, but they are a very useful way to track changes in the temperature of materials and reactions.

As the temperature increases, the liquid expands and the reading can be taken as the liquid moves up the stem. As the temperature decreases, the liquid contracts and moves down the stem.

TEST TUBES, FLASKS, BEAKERS, AND PIPETTES

All chemists use a range of tools and containers in their labs. It is important to know which is which, and what they are used for, so that you can set up your own experiments. If you have a chemistry set at home, you may have some of these already. Your science lab at school is sure to have them too.

TEST TUBES

If you think of a "mad professor" from an old film, they are nearly always shown clutching a bubbling test tube! In real life, test tubes are used to mix and store substances. They were first developed in the 1800s.

Test tubes are made of specially treated glass that is strong, and will not expand when it is heated. The glass is made heat resistant by adding an oxide of boron to the material it is made from.

Test tubes have curved bottoms, so are easy to wash out properly. That is important so that traces of chemicals do not stay behind in the tube and contaminate the next experiment.

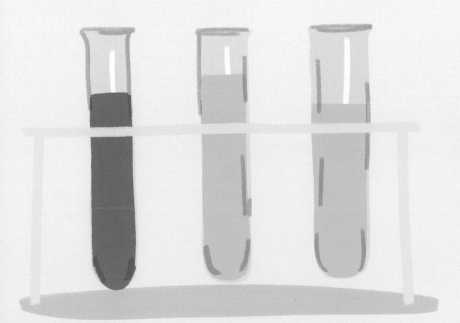

FLASKS

Flasks are also used to contain and mix substances. They are marked or "calibrated" with volumes down the side so that chemicals can be measured carefully into the flask.

Traditional cone-shaped flasks are sometimes called Erlenmeyer flasks after Emil Erlenmeyer, who invented them in 1860. They are useful as they can be swirled to mix chemicals without splashing the material on the scientist or the floor!

BEAKERS

Beakers are also calibrated containers that can be used to mix materials and to measure out liquids for experiments.

They come in lots of different sizes. Glass rods are used to stir materials in beakers to mix them together. Glass is used because it does not react with the chemicals.

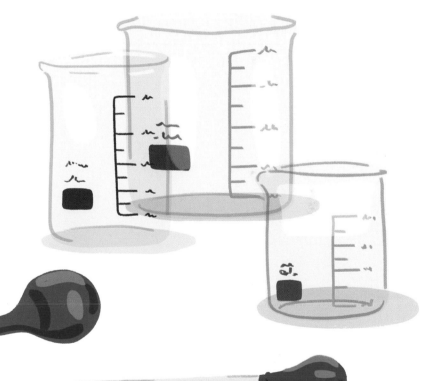

PIPETTES

Pipettes are glass tubes with a squeezy rubber top. They are used to add liquid to experiments drop by drop. You may have seen pipettes in bottles of cosmetic oil. Pipettes give the chemist control over the fluid they are adding when tiny quantities are needed. Some scientists even use tiny micropipettes in their work.

93

Have you ever made filter coffee, or seen it made in a café?
The process allows water to run through the filter paper,
taking the taste of coffee with it—but leaving the
coffee grounds behind.

 ## FILTRATION

In a lab, filters are used to separate solids from liquids or gases. The mixture is poured over a
filter, which catches particles. The filtered liquid—or filtrate—passes through the filter and is
collected in the beaker or flask beneath. The solid—or residue—is left behind in the filter paper.

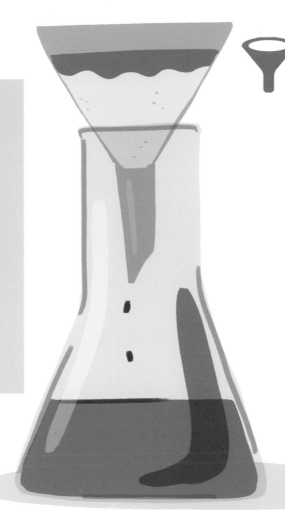

MIXTURES

Filters separate substances that are mixtures, which are not chemically "joined." The solid is also not soluble (cannot dissolve) in the liquid. An example of such a mixture is sand in water. Filtration is an example of a physical method of separation.

A funnel is used to separate mixtures. A filter paper is put into the cone of the filter to catch the solids. The liquid flows into a beaker.

EVAPORATION

Evaporation is a method that can be used to separate a dissolved solid from a liquid. Imagine that you had sandy seawater that you wanted to separate. You could filter out the sand, but not the salt from the water. The salt and water would be a solution. The water would be a solvent and the salt would be a solute. You could use heat to evaporate the solution. As the water evaporates, the salt crystals are left behind. This process is called crystallization.

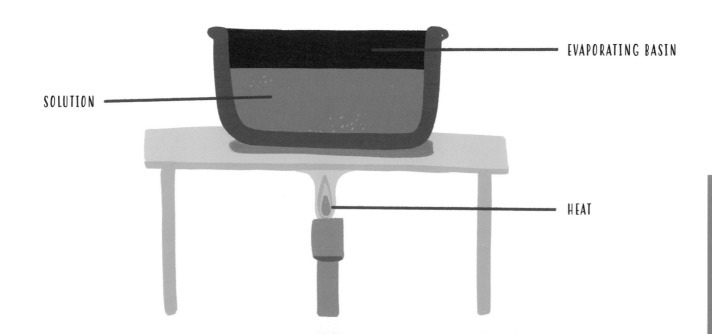

EVAPORATING BASIN

SOLUTION

HEAT

DISTILLATION

Distillation is used to separate and purify materials, including different liquids. Simple distillation separates solvents from solutions. For example, it could be used to separate salt from water. The solution is heated and the water evaporates, only to be collected and cooled in a separate container. The salt stays behind.

COOLING TUBE

PURE WATER IN GAS FORM

SALTY WATER

HEAT

FRACTIONAL DISTILLATION

Fractional distillation can be used to separate a mixture of two or more liquids.

Every liquid has a slightly different boiling point—where it turns from a liquid to a gas. Distillation harnesses this fact. It has been used since ancient times to create and purify alcoholic drinks and medicines.

BOILING POINTS

Distillation allows the liquid with the lowest boiling point to be collected first. For example, a mixture of ethanol and water could be separated in this way as ethanol has a lower boiling point than water. As the ethanol vapor rises, it is caught in a cool flask or beaker, and the vapor cools to become liquid again.

CRUDE OIL

Fractional distillation is used by the oil industry to separate crude oil into separate component liquids such as petroleum, bitumen, and diesel.

A tall fractionating column is fitted above the crude oil and condensers are fitted at different heights up the side of the column.

The crude oil is evaporated and the vapors condense at different temperatures in the fractionating column. This means they can be separated and collected for use.

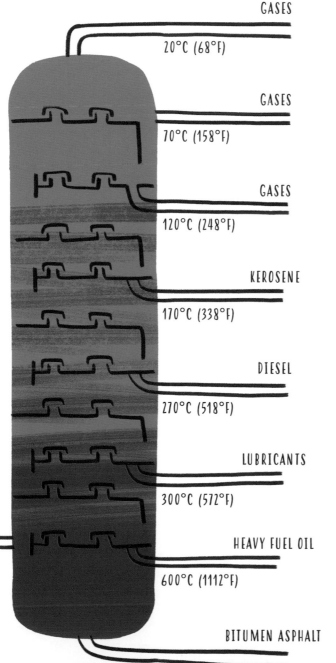

GASES
20°C (68°F)

GASES
70°C (158°F)

GASES
120°C (248°F)

KEROSENE
170°C (338°F)

DIESEL
270°C (518°F)

LUBRICANTS
300°C (572°F)

HEAVY FUEL OIL
600°C (1112°F)

BITUMEN ASPHALT

DOMESTIC GAS, PETROCHEMICALS, AND FEEDSTOCK

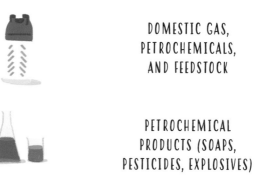

PETROCHEMICAL PRODUCTS (SOAPS, PESTICIDES, EXPLOSIVES)

CAR GASOLINE

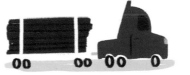

JET FUEL, KEROSENE FOR LIGHTING AND HEATING

DIESEL FUELS

LUBRICANTS, WAXES, AND POLISHES

FUEL FOR SHIPS AND BOILERS

ASPHALT FOR ROADS AND ROOFING

CHROMATOGRAPHY

Chromatography is a way of separating complex mixtures so they can be analyzed. It is used by forensic scientists to solve crimes! Chromatography can be used to create DNA "fingerprints" which help to identify criminals from substances collected at a crime scene.

SEPARATION

The word "chromatography" comes from the Greek words for color (*chroma*) and writing (*graph*). The experiments you can carry out with chromatography can be very colorful. The parts of the mixtures being separated move at different speeds through the medium used (such as chromatography paper), and this separates them.

TRY IT YOURSELF

You can see chromatography for yourself. Take a piece of filter paper (you can buy this cheaply) and cut a strip. Draw a big dot with a felt pen at one end of the paper and dip the nearest end in water. Leave it overnight.

In the morning you will see that, as the water has soaked up the strip, the ink has separated into different shades. The different components of the mixture separate at different speeds and you can see a trace of different shades in a streak up the paper. You can try the experiment again with drops of food coloring.

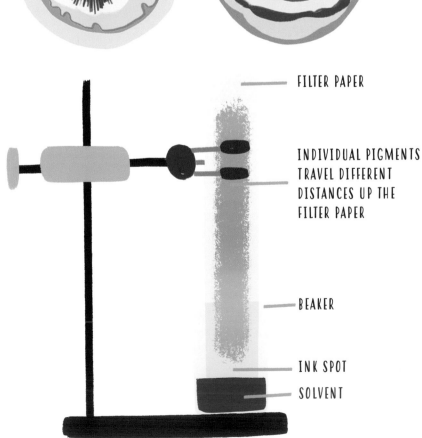

FILTER PAPER

INDIVIDUAL PIGMENTS TRAVEL DIFFERENT DISTANCES UP THE FILTER PAPER

BEAKER

INK SPOT

SOLVENT

THIN LAYER CHROMATOGRAPHY

In labs today, paper chromatography has been largely replaced, even though it's fun to do at home. Instead, chemists use thin layer chromatography.

Instead of paper, this technique uses a thin layer of a medium such as silica gel or cellulose. It is more efficient than paper chromatography. The shades run more quickly, and the separation is better and clearer. This leads to more accurate results.

COLUMN CHROMATOGRAPHY

Column chromatography separates compounds using chemicals as solvents. The compounds to be separated are dissolved in the solvent. The chromatography column is a glass or plastic tube packed with material such as silica gel, which is soaked in the solvent and then drained.

The solution with the compounds is then added in small amounts, so it soaks into the packing material. Fresh solvent is added to wash the compounds down through the column. The compounds wash through at different speeds and are separated.

GAS CHROMATOGRAPHY

Gas chromatography is also used to separate substances. The substance is turned into a gas and passed through a column in a "carrier" gas. This is an inert gas that does not react in the process, such as nitrogen.

As the substance is carried through the column it is separated into different components or parts. The column is inside an oven and the temperature is controlled to allow the individual components to leave the column at different times.

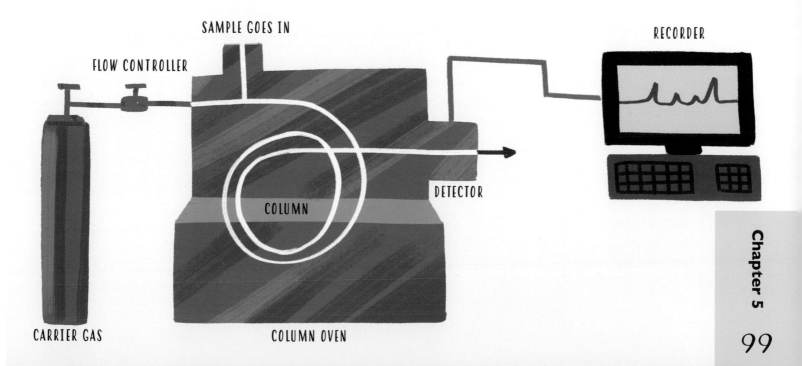

FLOW CONTROLLER · SAMPLE GOES IN · RECORDER · COLUMN · DETECTOR · CARRIER GAS · COLUMN OVEN

CHEMICAL REACTIONS

Chemical reactions happen when two reactants combine to form one or more products. "Reactants" is just the name scientists use for the substances that make a chemical reaction. They are used up during the reaction. The "products" are the new substances formed by the reaction.

REACTIONS EVERYWHERE

Chemical reactions happen all the time, everywhere in day to day life. Wood or coal burning on a fire is an example of a reaction. Metal rusting—that's a reaction, too.

When batteries provide electricity, it's due to a chemical reaction. When plants harness the energy from the sun using the process of photosynthesis—that's a reaction taking place in nature.

Chemical reactions even take place right inside you! Every time you eat, your body uses chemical reactions to break down the food so you can use the nutrients.

REACTION RATE

Not all reactions take place at the same speed, or rate. Some happen very quickly, and can cause explosions. Others, like metal rusting, can take years. The speed of the reaction is called the reaction rate. Reaction rates can be changed by adding energy to the reaction in the form of heat or electricity.

For rusting to occur, both water and oxygen must be present. Sometimes, people try to slow the reaction rate. Painting iron and steel bridges is one way to do this. It works by stopping water and oxygen from reaching the metal.

DON'T REACT!

Sometimes, it's important to make sure that reactions *don't* take place. For example, metal medical instruments are made from alloys (combinations of metals) that do not rust. This is important as they are often in damp situations—and rust in a wound would be dangerous.

REACTIVITY SERIES

Some metals are more reactive than others. They can be placed in the order of reactivity called the reactivity series.

Some metals, such as potassium and sodium, are *so* reactive that they need to be stored in oil to stop them from reacting to the moisture in the air!

MOST REACTIVE

POTASSIUM	K
SODIUM	Na
CALCIUM	Ca
MAGNESIUM	Mg
ALUMINUM	Al
ZINC	Zn
IRON	Fe
TIN	Sn
LEAD	Pb
COPPER	Cu
SILVER	Ag
GOLD	Au
PLATINUM	Pt

LEAST REACTIVE

OUT OF CURIOSITY

Your body can carry out thousands of different chemical reactions, and it is doing many of them all day and night.

🔥 COMBUSTION 🔥

Combustion is a special type of chemical reaction that happens when fuel combines with oxygen in air. It is called an exothermic reaction, which means it gives off heat. It also gives off light. When a substance is burned, it reacts with the oxygen in air to create a new substance called an oxide.

When magnesium is burned, it combines with the oxygen in air to create the compound magnesium oxide.

When wood burns on a fire, the oxygen in the air reacts with the stored carbon in the wood, creating ash and charcoal.

🔥 GREENHOUSE GASES

When fossil fuels such as coal, natural gas, and oil are burned, they combine with the oxygen in air to create carbon monoxide, carbon dioxide, and sulfur dioxide. These toxic gases are very damaging to Earth's atmosphere.

They are greenhouse gases, which speed climate change. Sulfur dioxide also causes acid rain, which is damaging to buildings, plants, and animal life.

 TRAVEL

Without combustion, it would be harder to travel. Car engines work by combustion. The fuel in a car catches fire and explodes in cylinders inside the engine repeatedly to push them up and down to propel the car.

Even space rockets could not travel without combustion! The rocket fuel combusts and the gases produced shoot out of the back of the rocket's engine, pushing the rocket forward.

 POLLUTION

When a substance burns and oxidization is not complete, tiny particles of soot— black carbon—are left behind. This causes pollution and dirty air.

 FLAMMABLE

An ignition point is the temperature at which a substance starts to burn. If a substance can be ignited in air, it is said to be flammable (or, confusingly, inflammable).

Combustion is useful to humans as it gives us heat and light, but those beautiful flames can quickly get out of control. Always be careful around fire!

FIREWORKS

Have you ever seen a firework display? Those sparkling lights and explosions happen because of chemical reactions! In rockets, the solid chemicals are packed inside tubes. Heat is added when the fireworks are lit. This **activation energy** starts the chemical reaction.

The chemicals burn or **combust** in the oxygen in the air. We call this an **exothermic** reaction. It gives off heat. The chemicals release gases like carbon monoxide and nitrogen. Fireworks also produce a lot of smoke as unburned particles fly around.

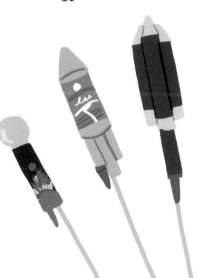

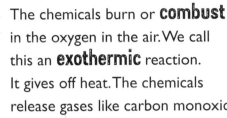

HOW ARE FIREWORKS DIFFERENT SHADES?

Fireworks contain metal compounds or salts. Different **compounds** give different shades of flames. Barium and copper salts burn with green and blue flames. Sodium burns yellow and orange. Strontium and calcium salts burn red.

?

OUT OF CURIOSITY

Although we do not know for sure, historians think that fireworks were invented in China in around 800 CE. Alchemists were trying to find a way to make people live forever—but they invented gunpowder by mistake along the way! They called it "*huo yao*," which means "fire chemical." They packed the powder into tubes and threw them in the fire to make explosions.
These early "bangers" developed to become fireworks!

FLARES

Fireworks are fun, but their technology is used in practical ways too. Flares are used to send up distress signals. They help people to be found when they are in trouble.

Flares are used by mountain rescue squads. They are also used at sea when boats are in trouble. Soldiers use flares to show their position. Flares often contain magnesium. If a person fires a flare from a flare gun, they want to be seen. Magnesium burns very brightly and burns for longer than the salts used in fireworks. Chemistry helps people to be rescued!

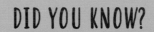

FLARE →

DID YOU KNOW?
The largest ever firework display was held in the Philippines in 2016. It used 800,000 fireworks!

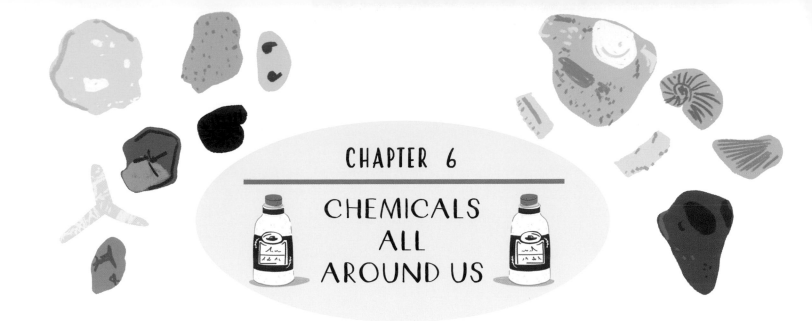

CHAPTER 6

CHEMICALS ALL AROUND US

As you have seen, everything in the world is made up of chemicals. Most of those chemicals are compounds, which are combinations of different elements. Some of those compounds are very complicated, with lots of different atoms, such as the chemicals in living things, including you.

You are now in a good position to spot chemicals in the world around you. Most animals take the chemical world as they find it, eating food and breathing in the air. Humans have gone far beyond that to use the world around us as a source of raw materials. We mine metals from the ground and mix them into alloys. We use chemical reactions to make entirely new chemicals, such as plastics, that don't occur naturally. We have made chemicals that help our plants to grow (fertilizers) and to change the taste of foods or keep them for longer (preservatives). We also use the chemicals in fossil fuels to provide energy for many different activities.

Humans use the resources of Earth like a vast chemistry set—often with good results, but sometimes with bad effects, too.

AIR

Air is made up of several different gases, including nitrogen (around 78%), oxygen (around 21%), and a small percentage of carbon dioxide (0.04%), along with a tiny amount of hydrogen and neon. Without air, we could not live on Earth—we need it to breathe.

THE ATMOSPHERE

Air surrounds the Earth, in a layer that is held in place by Earth's gravity. This blanket of gases is called the atmosphere. Near the surface of the Earth, the atmosphere is around 75% nitrogen and around 20% oxygen.

Greenhouse gases and ozone help to keep the planet warm and protect living things from dangerous radiation that comes from the Sun's rays.

THANKS!

The fact that we now have oxygen in the air is due to simple living things called cyanobacteria that developed in the oceans billions of years ago. They make their food by photosynthesizing. Since photosynthesis makes oxygen, cyanobacteria were responsible for putting large amounts of oxygen into Earth's atmosphere.

Over 2.5 billion years ago, the atmosphere was made up of an unbreathable mixture of carbon dioxide (CO_2) and gases that belched from volcanoes, such as methane and ammonia.

POLLUTION

Air also contains aerosol particles—tiny airborne specks of things like dust, pollen, soot, car exhaust, and smoke. This causes air pollution. There are megatons of it in the atmosphere!

The air also contains tiny bioaerosols, microbes that are carried along on the air via wind or a sneeze or cough.

OUT OF CURIOSITY

**Air is 'light," but there is a lot of it pushing down on the surface of the Earth. We call that air pressure.
Air pressure is highest at sea level, and lowest on high mountains.**

HUMIDITY

Air contains lots of water in gas form. Have you ever heard the word humid? It describes hot, damp air that contains lots of water.

High humidity can make it harder to breathe easily. Humidity is measured in percentages—you can see it on many weather forecasts. When humidity is 100%—it rains!

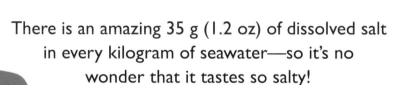

≋ SEAWATER ≋

Have you ever tasted salty seawater on your lips after swimming?
Or seen sparkly white salt on your skin as you dried in the sun?
Seawater is salty because of the minerals that are worn away from
rocks by rivers and raindrops, collecting in the sea.

The salt that is dissolved in the water can be extracted by
evaporation. When the water evaporates, sea salt (made up
of sodium chloride—NaCl—and small amounts of minerals)
is left behind—delicious sprinkled on your chips and fries.

There is an amazing 35 g (1.2 oz) of dissolved salt
in every kilogram of seawater—so it's no
wonder that it tastes so salty!

≋ GETTING SALTY

When the oceans first formed 3.8 billion years
ago, they were freshwater. Some of the ocean's
salts, including sodium, chlorine, and potassium,
came from underwater eruptions. Rain mixed
with carbon dioxide in the air to make a weak
acid that wore away rocks that also contained
salts. Rain and rivers carried salt into
the oceans.

THE DEAD SEA

Things float more easily in seawater than freshwater, which makes swimming easier! Any material can float if it is less dense than the liquid it is in. One of the saltiest natural bodies of water is the Dead Sea, bordered by Jordan, Israel, and the West Bank. In Arabic, the sea is called Al-Bahr Al-Mayyit , or "The Sea of Death." Sounds spooky!

In reality, the name comes from the fact that most things cannot live in such salty water. Any fish carried down rivers into the Dead Sea die off quickly; only some forms of bacteria can live there. It's a great place for swimmers though, as the dense water helps people to float easily.

FREEZING

Seawater freezes at a lower temperature than freshwater because salt lowers its freezing point. It freezes at around -2 °C (28.4 °Fahrenheit), instead of freshwater's 0 °Celsius (32 °Fahrenheit). The sea does freeze near the poles, where the temperature is very low. The polar ice cap at the North Pole is made of frozen seawater.

 # ROCK

Rock is a solid that makes up all of Earth's outer layer, which is called the crust—and without rock, there would be no land to live on! Have you ever looked closely at different types of rock? A good place to look is on the beach. That's because rocks from lots of different places are carried along by the action of waves to be deposited on pebbly beaches.

MINERALS

Minerals are solids that form naturally in the ground or in water. They sometimes contain a single element but are usually compounds. Rocks are mixtures of minerals.

Many rocks are made up of little grains. They can be broken back down into grains too, when sand is made. Rocks at the surface of the Earth are eroded by water, weather, and even wind. Next time you are at the beach, look very closely at a pinch of sand.

You could look with a magnifier for a closer view. You'll see many tiny specks of different rocks in each pinch of sand.

Rocks are formed in different ways. They are classified into three main groups , depending on the way they were made: sedimentary, metamorphic, and igneous.

SEDIMENTARY

Sedimentary rock is made when sand, mud, or the remains of living things become stuck together as they settle. Fragments drift down through water and create a tightly pressed mixture that hardens to become rock.

Sandstone is a sedimentary rock made from grains of broken rock. Mudstone and shale are made from hardened mud, while chalk is made from the shells of tiny ocean creatures. Fossils are found in sedimentary rock. They were made when dead creatures sank to the bottom of a body of water or mud and gradually their tissues were replaced by minerals.

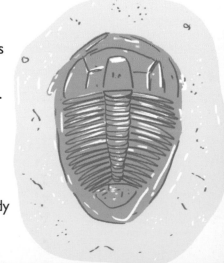

IGNEOUS

Igneous rock is formed when molten rock, heated inside the Earth, cools. Magma is the name for molten rock inside the Earth. Molten rock is called lava when it comes out of volcanoes.

If it cools underground, magma will cool slowly. That gives **crystals** time to develop. A crystal is a mineral with an ordered structure. When magma cools underground, it forms intrusive igneous rock. These rocks often have large crystals that you can see with the naked eye. An example of this type of igneous rock is granite.

When lava erupts from a volcano, then cools and hardens into rock, it forms volcanic rock—or what scientists call extrusive igneous rocks. When lava cools quickly, crystals do not have time to grow. Basalt is a volcanic rock with small crystals. Obsidian, another volcanic rock, does not have crystals at all. There are more than 700 types of igneous rock!

METAMORPHIC

Metamorphic rock is created when the pressure and heat in the Earth's crust cause changes in the minerals that rock is made from. That's how they get the name "metamorphic"—think of the way that a tadpole changes into a frog when it undergoes metamorphosis to remind you.

Metamorphic rocks started out as sedimentary, igneous, or metamorphic rocks. An example of a well-known metamorphic rock is marble, which is the metamorphized version of limestone.

OUT OF CURIOSITY

"Ore" is the name given to rocks that contain useful minerals, metals, and gems.

LAVA

MAGMA

MINERALS

Minerals are solids that occur naturally in the environment. They make up rocks. Minerals, unlike rocks, have a chemical structure that is the same throughout. They can be made of a single element, such as gold (Au) or copper (Cu). They can also be made up of a combination of elements. Scientists who study minerals are called mineralogists.

INORGANIC

Minerals are inorganic—that means they are not living organisms such as animals or plants. They usually have a crystal structure. There are many types of minerals but they are mainly divided by scientists into two groups, silicates and non-silicates. Silicates contain silicon and oxygen, and make up a huge 90% of Earth's crust.

Non-silicates include:

OXIDES

Chromite ($FeCr_2O_4$) is an oxide mineral made from oxygen (O), chromium (Cr), and iron (Fe).

CARBONATES

Calcium carbonate ($CaCO_3$) is a carbonate mineral that is found in coral skeletons and the shells of snails and oysters.

SULFIDES

One sulfide mineral is pyrite (FeS_2), which is made up of sulfur and iron (Fe). Pyrite is also called fool's gold because it looks a little like gold.

HALIDES

The salt we sprinkle on our dinner (NaCl) is a halide. It is made from the halogen chlorine (Cl) and sodium (Na).

MOHS HARDNESS SCALE

INCREASING HARDNESS

1) TALC

2) GYPSUM

3) CALCITE

4) FLUORITE

5) APATITE

6) ORTHOCLASE FELDSPAR

7) QUARTZ

8) TOPAZ

9) CORUNDUM

10) DIAMOND

Minerals are described by scientists according to their properties:

HARDNESS

Scientists use the Mohs scale to describe how hard a mineral is on a scale of 1–10, with 1 being the softest and 10 the hardest. If a mineral can be easily scratched, it is soft. If it cannot, like diamond, it is hard (in fact, the hardest mineral) and therefore a 10 on the Mohs scale.

LUSTER

Luster means how well minerals reflect light. A mineral might be described as dull, metallic, brilliant, or glassy.

SPECIFIC GRAVITY

Specific gravity (SG) is the density of the mineral. The mineral is always compared to water, which has an SG of 1. Quartz, for example, has an SG of 2.7.

STREAK

Streak is exactly that—the mark made when the mineral is rubbed across a rough surface such as a tile. The shade of the powder left behind is the streak. Weirdly, some minerals have a streak that is a different shade than their body!

CLEAVAGE

This means what happens when the mineral breaks into pieces. According to their structure, some may break into sheets and others into small cube-like shapes.

SHADE

Different minerals have different shades, depending on the elements they contain! The same mineral, such as corundum, can be shaded differently by the inclusion of tiny amounts of impurities—forming ruby or sapphire.

OUT OF CURIOSITY

A gem is a rare mineral such as emerald, ruby, sapphire, or diamond, that is cut and polished—and often worn as decoration.

FOSSIL FUELS: OIL

Oil is a fossil fuel. It's made up of the remains of plants and animals that died many millions of years ago. **Plankton** and plants died and fell to the bottom of the seas. Over millions of years these plant and animal remains were buried under layers and layers of mud and sand. The pressure and heat gradually changed these remains into oil.

The layers of mud and silt above the crude oil turn into shale rock due to the forces applied to them. The oil is forced up through cracks in the shale until it reaches rock it cannot travel though, called reservoir rock. The oil gathers here until it is discovered and extracted. Oil is often found in beds of fossilized shellfish that swam in ancient seas.

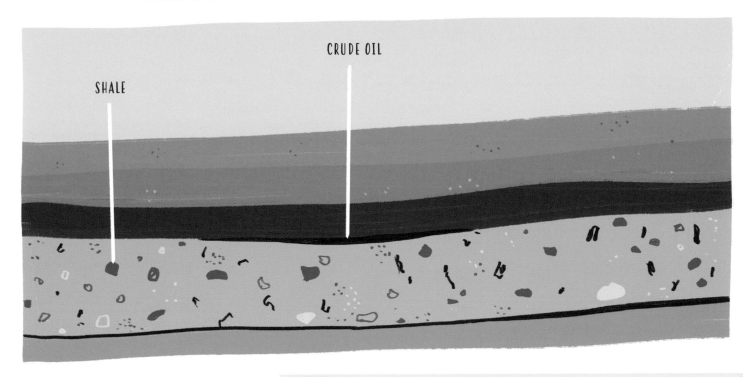

CRUDE OIL

SHALE

OIL

Geologists carry out seismic surveys (sending shock waves through rock) to find oil. They then do test drills to make sure oil is present in commercial quantities—that there is enough oil to make it worth extracting.

CRUDE OIL

Crude oil is extracted from the ground as a thick black liquid. It is made up of hydrocarbons. Hydrocarbons are chain molecules made from hydrogen and carbon atoms. These hydrocarbons are separated by distillation into thick polymers (such as those used to make plastic), which are less flammable, and volatile fuels, which are highly flammable. Polymers are large chain molecules made by the joining together of many smaller molecules, end to end.

Volatile fuels made from crude oil include:

PETROLEUM	DIESEL
KEROSENE	JET FUEL

LIQUID PETROLEUM GAS (LPG)

 PIPELINES

Oil is easy to transport along great pipelines. This carries problems of its own though as there has been controversy about the environmental impact of large pipes running through natural areas.

 WHERE IN THE WORLD?

Lots of the oil in the world comes from Saudi Arabia, Russia, parts of the USA, China, Iran, and Iraq. It is also drilled for from great platforms which extract oil from under the seabed of the North Sea.

 MAKING ELECTRICITY

Oil reacts with oxygen to combust. Combustion releases energy which can be used to drive engines and to provide heat and light.

Oil can even be used to create electricity! The oil is burned to heat water and produce steam. Steam powers a turbine, and the blades of the turbine spin. The turbine is attached to a generator, which uses the power to generate electricity. Electricity produced in this way is more expensive than electricity produced by burning coal and gas.

GREENHOUSE GASES

Oil is a fossil fuel, and when fossil fuels are burned they produce carbon dioxide—a greenhouse gas. Sadly, producing greenhouse gases contributes to climate change and pollution.

Oil is a non-renewable source of energy—we can't make more. Once it is gone, that's it! Crude oil is used in the production of a huge amount of consumer products, including plastics. When crude oil runs out, industry will need alternatives.

🏭 FOSSIL FUELS: COAL 🏭

Coal was made from the remains of plants in ancient swampy forests. When the plants died, they fell into the swamp and got buried under layers of silt and mud. The pressure of these layers, as more and more formed, slowly turned the remains into coal.

An amazing 4 billion tonnes (4.4 billion tons) of coal is mined from the ground every year. It is found in many places around the world, including Australia, China, northern England, India, Poland, Russia, Scotland, Wales, and the USA.

 MAKING ELECTRICITY

Coal is burned to release energy in the form of heat. It is the world's largest single source of energy for electricity, producing around 40%. Coal is burned in a furnace, which heats a boiler. The boiler produces steam, which spins turbines to create electricity.

Coal is not a renewable source of energy, because once it has been consumed we cannot make more. This fossil fuel produces greenhouse gases such as sulfur dioxide (SO_2) and carbon dioxide (CO_2) when burned, which contribute to climate change. It also creates acid rain and can contaminate water supplies.

 CARBON

Coal is made from carbon (C). It also contains small amounts of elements such as oxygen (O), hydrogen (H), nitrogen (N), and sulfur (S). Different types of coal contain different amounts of carbon.

Anthracite is a type of coal that is very hard and shiny. It burns with a blue flame, and is made up of 86–98% carbon. Anthracite is different from most other types of coal because it is found in metamorphic rocks, whereas other coal, such as lignite, is associated with sedimentary rocks. Lignite contains around 75% carbon.

 COAL MINERS

Mining is a dangerous occupation due to risks of mine collapse and lung damage.

FOSSIL FUELS: NATURAL GAS

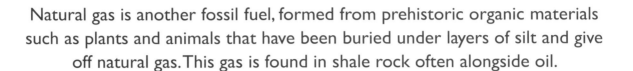

Natural gas is another fossil fuel, formed from prehistoric organic materials such as plants and animals that have been buried under layers of silt and give off natural gas. This gas is found in shale rock often alongside oil.

Natural gas is clear and lighter than air. Sometimes it escapes through cracks in the ground and catches fire. It is thought that people discovered natural gas as a fuel by seeing these naturally occurring fires. Today, **geologists** look for natural gas in shale rock, then dig test wells in likely places.

FRACKING

Hydraulic fracking is a controversial way to extract natural gas. Fracking creates forced fractures or breaks in rock layers by using pressurized fluid. This forces up natural gas (and sometimes, oil) from the shale.

By 2010, 60% of new gas and oil wells worldwide were using hydraulic fracturing to force new channels into rock to make it easier to extract the fuels. Fracking is now used around the world.

Fracking makes the extraction of gases cheaper—but it is very harmful to the environment. It can cause the contamination of groundwater, and can cause damage to layers of rock under a large area of land.

It also affects air quality by bringing other chemicals, which may be harmful, to the surface. Many countries have now banned fracking.

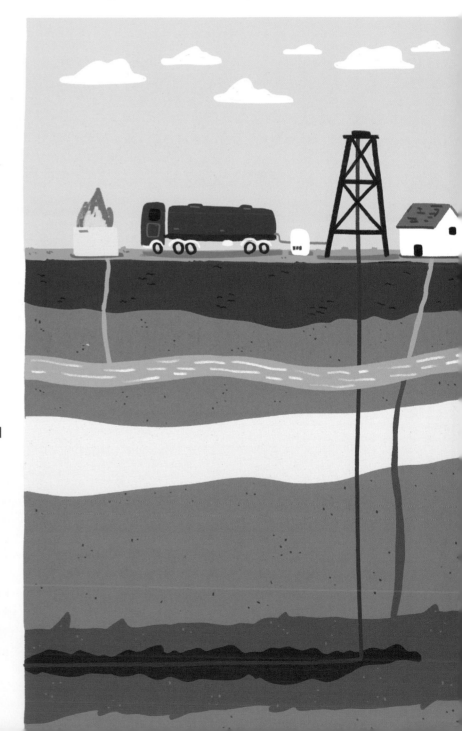

STINKY!

Natural gas is made up of many different gases, including methane (CH_4), carbon dioxide (CO_2), butane (C_4H_{10}), propane (C_3H_8), and nitrogen (N). Natural gas has no natural smell, but a smelly substance is added to it for safety—so that people can smell a gas leak!

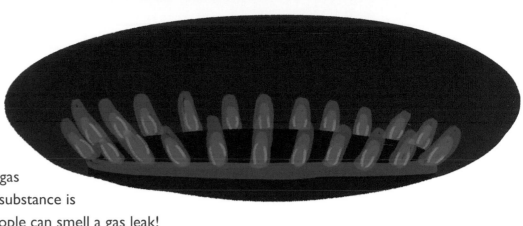

GAS POWERED

Natural gas reacts with oxygen to combust, which releases energy. Natural gas is used in many homes for heating and cooking. Some power plants use natural gas to create electricity. Heat from the burning gas powers a turbine, which runs a generator that turns movement energy into electrical energy.

The waste heat produced can also be used to heat water, which in turn can produce steam to drive more generators—and create more electricity! That is an efficient use of a finite resource. Natural gas is also used to make products such as fertilizer and plastics.

EXTRACTION

When natural gas is extracted from the ground, it also contains water, other chemicals, and even oil. These must be removed before the gas is ready to be used.

PIPELINES

Natural gas is moved via underground pipelines. The laying of pipelines can have an impact on the environment. Extraction also damages the environment as wildlife and plant life are disrupted.

WHERE IN THE WORLD?

Natural gas was first found in the Middle East, in Iran. Today, it is extracted in many parts of the world, including Africa, Eastern Europe, Russia, North and South America, the North Sea, and the Irish Sea.

This fossil fuel is not a renewable source of energy. Once it is used up, there will be no more.

GREENHOUSE GASES

Natural gas, like other fossil fuels, produces greenhouse gases that contribute to climate change. It has, however, been called the "cleanest" of the fossil fuels as it produces little in the way of other types of pollution.

METALS

The science of studying metals is called metallurgy. Metals are strong but flexible solids that are often found in rock ore, which is dug from the ground in great mines. To separate the metal from ore, the rock is crushed and heated to high temperatures in a process called smelting.

PROPERTIES

Metals are great conductors of heat and electricity—but some metals such as copper are especially conductive so they are used in electrical circuits. Conducting allows electricity to pass through a material. Metals are usually sonorous—they make a noise like a bell when they are struck.

Metals are malleable, which means they can be beaten into a thin sheet. They are also ductile, so they can be stretched out into thin wires. Metal is strong, so it is made into things like bridges and cars—and even coins, so they do not wear away with lots of use.

BONDS

It is their very strong, metallic bonds (the force that binds the atoms together) that give metals their properties of bendability and conductivity.

All metals are solids at room temperature, apart from mercury (Hg), which is a liquid. Their strong bonds also give most metals a high melting point. However, they can be melted to pour into molds to make components, tools, machinery, and electronics.

There are different types of metals:

BASE METALS

These reactive metals corrode (or break down) easily in the air. Oxidation happens when the metal combines with the oxygen in the air. Examples of base metals are zinc (Zn), copper (Cu), lead (Pb), and tin (Sn).

Did you know that "tin" cans are in fact made from several metals? Most drink cans—75% around the world—are made from aluminum. Most food cans are made from steel plated with tin or chromium.

When copper corrodes it turns a blue-green shade. This is oxidation taking place. It's a chemical reaction where the copper reacts with the oxygen in air to create copper oxide.

In ancient times, Romans and Greeks corroded copper on purpose and used the green shade, called verdigris, as a pigment for paints and dyes.

NOBLE METALS

Noble metals are unreactive metals such as platinum (Pt), gold (Au), iridium (Ir), palladium (Pd), and silver (Ag).

They resist corrosion and oxidation, and because they are quite rare they are valuable. They are often made into necklaces, earrings, and rings or used in technology.

FERROUS METALS

Ferrous metals are iron and alloys of iron. Iron is attracted to magnets so ferrous metals are too. Examples of ferrous metals are steel, cast iron, and pig iron. Steel is mainly made from iron (Fe), carbon (C), and manganese (Mn).

⚙ ALLOYS ⚙

Alloys are metals that combine two or more elements. They are mixtures, made to combine the properties of different metals. They are produced to make stronger and corrosion-free metals for a variety of applications. Steel is one of the most useful and widely made alloys. Steel is made of iron, plus a variety of different ingredients. In industry and construction, steel is often made by combining iron and carbon.

Look around and you may find a type of steel in your cutlery drawer at home—this is stainless steel. It is made from steel and chromium, and is rust free and easy to clean.

⚙ ALUMINUM ALLOYS

You may have held this alloy in your hand today, if you have drunk soda from a can. Aluminum is combined with elements such as silicon and copper to make an alloy.

It doesn't corrode and it is very light, so it is perfect for packaging. It's useful for other things that need to be strong but light, such as ladders and airplanes.

 # BRASS

Brass is an alloy made from zinc and copper. You may have some in your house as it is often used to make ornaments and candlesticks.

 # GOLD

Most wearable gold you see is an alloy, too. Pure gold is very soft and easily damaged, so it is often mixed with other metals to make it stronger. Look in a jewelry shop window. Find the labels on the gold. The higher the number, the more gold is used in the alloy: 24 karat gold is pure gold, 18 karat gold is made with 75% gold, and 9 karat gold contains just 37.5% of pure gold.

OUT OF CURIOSITY

The first known alloy was made in ancient times—the Bronze Age! The Stone Age was before that, when people did not use metals. Bronze is a combination of tin and copper.

It was used to make tools, weapons, and utensils, as well as wearable art—and today, it is used for statues.

GLOSSARY

acid: An acid is a chemical with a low pH. Acids have a pH lower than 7.

alchemist: A person who studied how to change basic substances such as common metals into other substances such as gold. Alchemists also studied magic and astrology.

alkali: An alkali is any solution with a pH of more than 7. Alkali (or base) is the opposite of "acid."

atom: The smallest particle of a chemical element that can exist.

atomic number: The number of protons in each atom. The atomic number decides the position of an element on the periodic table.

base: Any solution with a pH of more than 7.

botanist: A scientist who studies plant life.

chemical reaction: A process in which one or more substances are converted to one or more different substances.

cell: Every living thing is made up of cells. A cell is the smallest unit with the properties of life. **chlorophyll:** A green pigment in plants that absorbs light and turns it into chemical energy, via a process called photosynthesis.

chromosome: A long DNA molecule found inside plant and animal cells which contains part or all of the genetic information for a living thing.

conduction: The process by which heat, electricity, or sound travels through material.

crystal: A solid material where the material it is made up of fits together in a repeating pattern. Common examples are table salt and sugar.

density: The space a substance takes up (its volume) in relation to the amount of matter in the substance (its mass). If a substance is small but heavy, it has high density.

dissolve: When a solid is mixed with a liquid and it seems to disappear, it is said to have dissolved.

distillation: A process where a mixture made up of liquids with different boiling points can be separated.

DNA: Deoxyribonucleic acid is a long molecule found in the cells that carries instructions for the structure and function of living things.

ductile: Can be hammered thin or stretched into wire without breaking.

electron: A negatively charged particle found in an atom.

element: A substance made of a single type of atom. An example would be iron.

evaporation: The process of changing from a liquid or solid state into a gas (like a puddle in sunshine).

exothermic: Describes a chemical change accompanied by a release of heat.

filtration: The process used to separate solid particles in a liquid or gaseous fluid. A filter allows fluids to pass through, but not solid particles.

forensic scientist: Looks at evidence (such as fingerprints, blood, and hair) to help solve crimes by using biology, chemistry, and physics.

formula: A chemical formula is the way scientists write down symbols to show the number and type of atoms present in a molecule.

gas: A state of matter. A gas flows like air. A gas can fill any container it is put inside as the molecules can move apart freely.

geologist: A scientist who studies rocks, minerals, and the layers of the Earth's surface

gravity: A force of attraction that exists between any two masses.

greenhouse gas: A gas in the atmosphere (such as carbon dioxide, nitrous oxide, and methane) that traps energy from the sun.

infrared radiation: A type of energy invisible to human eyes, but felt as heat.

insulation: Material used to stop electricity, heat, or sound passing from one conductor to another.

ion: An atom or molecule that carries an electric charge.

isotopes: Atoms that have the same number of electrons and protons, but different numbers of neutrons—so they have different physical properties.

lipid: A type of oily organic molecule found in living things.

liquid: A state of matter. Liquid molecules flow freely, like water, and take on the shape of containers they are put into.

lubricant: An oily, greasy, or slippery substance used to reduce rubbng between surfaces.

malleable: Bendy and able to change shape.

mass: The amount of matter in a substance.

matter: What everything in the Universe is made of. All matter is made up of tiny particles called atoms.

mineral: Naturally occurring inorganic solid with a defined chemical structure.

molecule: A group of two or more atoms that form the smallest unit into which a pure substance can be divided and still keep the chemical properties of the substance.

monomer: A small molecule that reacts with another to form a larger molecule.

nanoparticle: A small particle that the human eye cannot see. They sometimes have very different properties to larger amounts of a substance.

nanotechnology: The science that studies nanoparticles.

neutron: Tiny particles that are part of an atom. They have a neutral charge (are neither positive nor negative).

orbital: Orbitals are the places around the nucleus of an atom where electrons move around in a wave.

organism: A living thing.

oxidization: Any chemical reaction that involves the movement of electrons. The substance that loses electrons is said to be oxidized.

patent: A legal document that gives an inventor the right to be the only person to make and sell their invention for a number of years.

periodic table: The system used by scientists to arrange chemical elements.

pH: Almost all liquids are either acids or bases, on a pH scale of 0–14. From 0-7 are acids; from 7–14 are bases. Neutral substances such as pure water are 7 on the scale.

photosynthesize: A process that uses water, carbon dioxide, and energy from sunlight to produce food for plants in the form of glucose, a type of sugar.

pigment: Something that gives shade to a substance.

plankton: Tiny plants and animals that float in the sea and other bodies of water, such as lakes.

plasma: A state of matter. Created when energy is added to gas and some electrons break off and leave the atoms.

polymer: Very large, chain-like molecules.

proton: A positively charged particle found at the center of the atom in the nucleus.

radioactive: If a substance is radioactive, it gives off radiation—small particles of energy. Radiation is dangerous to living things as it can cause sickness and cell damage.

reactive: A measure of how easily a substance reacts with other substances.

respiration: The process living things use to create energy for living, involving an exchange of gases, oxygen, and carbon dioxide.

solid: A state of matter. In solids, molecules do not flow as they do in liquids and gases. Solids tend to keep their shape.

solution: Created when a substance dissolves in a liquid.

spectroscopy: The study of light shone through a solid, liquid, or gas. Spectroscopy allows scientists to study tiny things such as molecules, electrons, neutrons, and protons.

state of matter: Solid, liquid, gas, and plasma are states of matter. Matter takes a different form, depending on how its molecules are arranged.

ultraviolet: Short light waves produced by the Sun. People cannot see them, but some insects such as bees can.

volume: The amount of space an object takes up.

INDEX